There Were
Two Trees
In The Garden

By Rick Joyner

MorningStar Publications
P.O. Box 369
Pineville, NC 28134

Printed in the United States of America
Seventh printing. 80,000 copies in print.

International Standard Book Number: 1-878327-04-6

Distributed by:

MorningStar Publications
P.O. Box 369
Pineville, N.C. 28134

Table of Contents

1

The Two Trees

There were two trees in the Garden of Eden which challenged the course of the entire human race — the Tree of Knowledge of Good and Evil and the Tree of Life. These same two "trees" continue to challenge us. When one becomes a Christian, the challenges do not end — they may well increase. Many times we will have to choose between the fruit of these trees. Between them lies the focal point of the dichotomy between the Kingdom of God and the present evil age.

The Tree of Knowledge and the Tree of Life are symbolic of two spiritual lineages or "family trees". The Bible, from Genesis to Revelation, is a history of two lineages. Understanding these lineages can help us to understand the most common errors besetting the entire human race, including the Church.

Satan did not tempt Eve with the fruit of the Tree of Knowledge just because the Lord had put if off limits. He tempted her with it because the source of his power was rooted in that tree. Furthermore, the Lord did not make it taboo just to test his children; He prohibited the eating of its fruit because He knew it was poison. When He instructed Adam not to eat from the Tree of Knowledge, He didn't say "If you eat from that tree I'm going to kill you" but "On the day that you eat from it you will die." It was not *just* man's disobedience that brought death to the world; it was also the fruit from this tree.

The Tree of Knowledge of Good and Evil is the Law. As the Apostle Paul declared: *"The power of sin is the Law"* (1 Cor. 15:56). This is because through the Law we derive our knowledge of good and evil. We may wonder how this knowledge brings death until we see the fruit. The knowledge of good and evil kills us by distracting us from the One who is the source of life: the Tree of Life — Jesus. The Tree of Knowledge causes us to focus our attention upon ourselves. Sin is empowered by the law; not just because the evil is revealed but the good as well. It drives us either to corruption or self-righteousness. Both lead to death.

It is significant that this tree is found in the center of the garden (Gen. 3:3). Self-centeredness is the chief malady with which we become afflicted. After Adam and Eve ate its fruit, their first response was self-inspection. Before eating they had not even noticed their nakedness. Their attention was on the Lord and the purposes for which He had created them. After eating, the good and evil which they now understood forced them to measure themselves by it. There is no easier way to keep us from the Tree of Life than to have us focus our attention upon ourselves. This is what the Law accomplishes. Because of this Paul called it "the ministry of death" and the "ministry of condemnation" (2 Cor. 3:7,9).

When we define the Tree of Knowledge as the Law, we are not referring only to the Law of Moses. We often think of the Old Testament as the law and the New Testament as Grace, but this is not necessarily true. The Old Covenant is the Letter; the New Covenant is the Spirit. If we read the New Testament with an Old Covenant heart it will just be law to us. We'll have dead religion with righteousness that is based on compliance with written commandments instead of a living relationship with our God.

The Lord said He was going to send His Spirit to lead us into all truth. All truth is in Jesus, of whom the Spirit was sent to testify (Eph. 4:21). The Bible is a most precious and wonderful gift from the Lord to his people. But the Bible was not meant to take place of the Lord Himself, or the Spirit whom He sent. The Bible is a means, not an end. Knowing the book of the Lord is not our goal; our goal is to know the Lord of the book. The many errors and divisions within the body of Christ are not due to fault in the Bible, but our misuse of it. Some of the laws and principles we have wrested from the New Testament rival anything that the Pharisees did to the Old Testament! This has caused us to try to measure our spirituality by how well we conform to the letter. Our spirituality is not found in adapting to a form, but by the forming of Jesus within us.

It was for a good reason that the Lord instructed us to judge men by their fruit. One can teach a parrot to say and do the right things. Satan often comes as "an angel of light", proclaiming scriptures; and his work will often conform to the letter. But only Jesus can bring forth the fruit that is *LIFE*. *"The letter kills, but the spirit gives life"* (2 Cor. 3:6).

If we read the scriptures by the Spirit, they will testify of Jesus and will come to life. The scriptures are meant to be a testimony of Him. *"You search the scriptures because you think that in them you have eternal life; but it is these that bear witness of Me"* (John 5:39). The Spirit was sent to lead us to Him in the scriptures and everything else. Reading the scriptures without the Spirit brings only the knowledge of good and evil, which actually brings death. Satan can counterfeit form but he can never counterfeit the fruit of the Spirit — which is Jesus, the Tree of Life. Man is able, to a certain degree for various self-centered and deceptive reasons, to change his outward behavior. Only the Spirit can change a man's heart. Therefore, the Lord looks upon the hearts of men, and in them He is looking for the heart of His Son.

The Lord's first act of creation was to bring forth light. The very next thing He did was separate the light from darkness. There can be no cohabitation between light and darkness. When the Lord re-creates a man and he is born again, He immediately begins to separate the light from the darkness in his life. Almost inevitably, in our zeal for Him, we try to take over this work and perform it by the only way we have ever known — through the knowledge of good and evil. This struggle between law and grace — flesh and Spirit — is the source of much inner discord afflicting Christians.

On the third day of creation, the Lord established a physical and spiritual law that was critically important. He ordered that trees would only bear fruit after their own kind and produce seed after their own kind (Gen. 1:11-12). The fruit of these two trees is to forever be separate and distinct, as the Lord Jesus also testified.

> *For there is no good tree which produces bad fruit; nor a bad tree which produces good fruit. For each tree is known by its fruit* (Luke 6:43-44).

The Apostle Paul further testified: *"whatever a man sows, this he will also reap"* (Gal. 6:7). We cannot be partaking of the Tree of Knowledge and bring forth fruit that is life. Likewise, if we are partaking of the Tree of Life we will not bring forth the fruit of the Tree of Knowledge — death. A tree can only produce fruit after its own kind.

As mentioned earlier, trees in scriptures are often symbolic of family lineages. In order for Christ to come forth in man, His seed had to be sown in man. Likewise, in order for the "man of sin" to come forth in man, that seed also had to be sown in man. The fruit of a seed cannot be reaped unless it is first planted. When Adam and Eve ate of the Tree of Knowledge, they were destined to perpetuate the fruit of that tree; consequently death spread throughout their descendants. But God in His grace and mercy determined that He would redeem their mistake. He planted in man the seed that would again bring forth the Tree of Life in man — Jesus. Through Him true life would be restored to man. His seed is a spiritual seed, sown by the Holy Spirit through prophecy. No flesh could beget Him but all flesh could receive Him. The Lord promised transgressing woman that a seed would come forth from her that would crush the head of the serpent that had deceived her (Gen. 3:15). In the first two sons born to the woman, we discern the seeds of each tree.

2

Cain and Abel

After the transgression of our first parents, the Lord prophesied the propagation of the two seeds within man: those who would embrace the nature of the serpent and those who would be of the nature of Christ. Cain and Abel clearly reflect these seeds and their predicted enmity.

Cain

Cain is in us all. He was the firstborn and a type of "the first man, Adam". He was of the earth, *"a tiller of the ground"* (Gen. 4:2). This is a fundamental characteristic of those we will refer to as the seed of Cain — being "earthly-minded". This includes all who have not truly been born again by the Spirit. As the Lord Jesus testified *"Unless one is born again by the Spirit he cannot see the Kingdom of God"* (John 3:3). Just as the curse upon the serpent to crawl on his belly forces him to conform to the contour of the earth, so his seed is confined to the natural realm. *"A natural man does not accept the things of the Spirit of God; for they are foolishness to him, and he cannot understand them because they are spiritually appraised"* (1 Cor. 2:14). This is our condition until the curse is removed in Christ. As we are born again by His Spirit, we begin to see and walk in heavenly places, and become less and less subject to the contours of the natural realm.

The seed of Cain, in their restricted vision, became worshippers of the creature instead of the Creator. Cain is a "tiller of the ground" because that is all he can see. We can only worship that

11

which we know! The culminating stages of self-worship are evident in materialism and various humanistic dogmas. These philosophies place man at the center of the universe. "Religious" man, whose devotion is to the church or religious organizations rather than Jesus, is also a "creature-worshiper". This attitude is also found in spiritualists who seek betterment, fulfillment, harmony, etc. by seeking unity with the creation instead of the Creator.

In the conclusion of God's written word to man, the Book of Revelation, we see the consummation of the two seeds that were sown in man: "beast" and the glorified Christ. In the scriptures to this point, we see their development, but here we are given a glimpse of their conclusion. It is of utmost importance that we understand the development and final revelation of these two seeds.

The Revelation was not given to John only to unfold a coming sequence of events . . . it was given as a *"revelation of Jesus Christ"* (Rev. 1:1). We must see this to understand it properly. A sequence of events takes place in the vision, but these are given to reveal Christ. The apostle testified that these were *"things which must shortly take place"* (verse 1). Events began and continue to occur which perfectly corroborate his prophecy. The Revelation of John is a revelation of Jesus. The very word *history* originally meant "His-story". As the Spirit opens our eyes, even in what may appear to be the terrible confusion of man's history, we see Him and His purposes.

In John's vision, there is also a great deal about the anti-Christ, or the "man of sin". This man of sin is the personification of the **sin of man**. This is our basic nature until we are changed in Christ. This is the mature fruit of the Tree of Knowledge. The root and power of the man of sin is the serpent; the beast had to be fully revealed in man . . . whatever is sown must also be reaped. In this beast we see ourselves without Christ. By this revelation we begin to perceive the depth of the unfathomable grace and mercy of God and our profound need to be reborn in Christ.

Revelation 13:16-17 tells us that the beast has a mark which he attempts to place upon us. In chapter 14, verses 9-10, we see that terrible wrath comes upon all who take the mark. Men have striven to understand the manner in which this beast would attempt to place his mark on them so they would know what to refuse and be free from the wrath foretold. Many of those who are frantically trying to understand the manner in which the beast will try to place his mark on them are partaking of the *spirit* of the beast everyday! Will one be free from the curse of the mark if he refuses a physical mark but is of the very nature of the beast? Just as the seal (literal "mark") that the Lord places upon His bondservants is not a physical mark, the mark of the beast is probably far more subtle than we have been led to believe. Regardless of the form in which the mark comes (or has come), those who have partaken of the nature of the beast — the spirit of the world — will not be able to resist the mark or anything else from the beast. Our only deliverance from the wrath of God is to be found in Christ. Taking a mark is not a sin. The sin is found in worshipping the beast. The mark is merely evidence that one has been worshipping it.

John gave us a crucial exhortation in relation to this: *"Here is wisdom. Let him who has understanding calculate the number of the beast, for the number is that of a man; and his number is six hundred and sixty-six"* (Rev. 13:18). The number 666 is not taken arbitrarily. Because man was created on the sixth day, the number six is often used symbolically in scripture as the number of *man*. This number is further identification of the spirit of the beast, which is the spirit of fallen man. In verse 11 we see that this beast *"comes up out of the earth"*. This beast is the result of the seed of Cain being a "tiller of the ground" or earthly-minded. The beast is the embodiment of religion that originates in the mind of man. It comes up out of the earth, in contrast to Christ who comes down out of heaven. Jesus can only be brought forth by the Spirit of God. The New Jerusalem, typical of the true church, the bride of Christ, also comes down out of heaven, testifying of its heavenly origin. It is born of God, not man.

If one is trusting in his knowledge of good and evil to discern the beast, he will easily be deceived. The nature of the beast is rooted just as much in the "good" that is in man as it is in the evil. Satan comes as an "angel of light", or *messenger of truth*, because good has always been more deceptive than evil. It was not the evil nature of the Tree of Knowledge that deceived Eve; it was the good. The "good" of the Tree of Knowledge kills just as certainly as the evil.

The evil nature of man is being manifested in these last days with a greater and greater intensity, but so is the "good" of man that is rooted in the same tree. Just as the evil is becoming more blatant, the good is becoming more subtle and deceptive. What, for example, would the popularity of a leader be today if he promised safe streets, sound currency, an end to inflation, unemployment, pornography and all other forms of perversion, restoration of national dignity and military strength — **and delivered on all these promises?**

Adolph Hitler promised all of these things to a depression and war crippled Germany and delivered on every one of them. Milton Mayor, in *They Thought They Were Free*, observed, "Fascism came as an 'angel of light' and German Christians, both Protestant and Catholic, welcomed Hitler as a gift from God. Nazism was seen as redemptive of a decadent society; and came almost as a puritanism to a majority sick of perversions and license parading as liberty". Hitler actually used the church in Germany as a springboard to power.

It was basically the German churches' superficial understanding of redemption that opened the door to this terrible deception. The good that is in man will never redeem him from the evil that is in him. It is still the same tree, and its fruit will always be death. The system whose coming appeared so good to the German Christians shocked the world with its evil deeds, but its nature did not change. The good of man is just the other face of the evil in man. Satan uses good as a tool to bring about his purposes. There were only a relative handful of German Christians that discerned the deception from the beginning. The same Satanic mask is being promulgated today. Our discernment must be more than distinguishing good from evil; we must know the Lord's voice and follow Him only.

Milton Mayer added a significant insight into what happened in Germany preceding the war: "I felt and still feel that it was not just German man that I met, but MAN (emphasis mine). He happened to be in Germany under certain conditions. He might be here under certain conditions. He might, under certain conditions, be I." The truth is that the same beast is within us all. It is the Adamic nature that continually beckons us to eat of the Tree of Knowledge of Good and Evil.

Just because one claims to be a Christian does not mean that he is one. Some of the worst deceivers in history have pretended to come in His name. The Lord Himself warned, *"Many will come in*

My name saying I am the Christ, and will deceive many" (Matt. 24:5). Some have interpreted this as saying that many would come claiming to *be* the Christ and would deceive many, but that is not what He said. He warned that many would come declaring that He, Jesus, was indeed the Christ and yet be deceivers. History testifies that this has certainly been true. Compared to some of the popes that ruled the middle ages, Hitler would seem a choirboy. Some of the most abominable atrocities ever committed by man were done by those who claimed to be *the Church* during the middle ages. We forget history too quickly, and Satan continues to come as an angel of light.

As Christians we often gravitate toward, and esteem most highly, those who are the most conservative and moral. Jesus did not. Sinners did not crucify the Lord. Israel's most moral and upstanding citizens crucified Him. The Lord declared to such that the publicans and harlots would enter the Kingdom of God before they would. Those who consider themselves "good citizens" or "good moral people" may be further from the Kingdom than the lowest pervert. *"There is no one who does good, not even one!"* (Ps. 14:3). Sinners, and even the demon-possessed, humbled themselves before the Lord; the religious and upstanding citizens held Him in contempt as not being as righteous as they were. Who is the enemy? As I once heard a recently enlightened pastor remark, "We have met the enemy and *HE IS US!"*

There are many "good" causes being championed in the world today which frequently serve as distractions for the Christian as they draw our attention away from our true calling. In most cases there is no question that the issues are just and right, but they only deal with the symptoms . . . they leave the disease untouched. Homosexuality is a flagrant perversion, but it is only a symptom of a much deeper problem. Abortion is a horror, but it too is just a symptom. Even communism in its most cruel and oppressive forms is but a symptom of the disease that afflicts the soul of man. For centuries the church has been offering the world band-aids for a deep, mortal wound. What man needs is more than just behavioral changes. We must stop flailing at the branches and put an ax to the root of the tree.

Man's nature must change. In every man and woman born, there is the nature of the beast which seeks to draw all attention and worship to itself. Even the greatest compassion and benevolence of man is often an attempt to atone for his own evil and justify why he does not need Christ and His atonement. The Good of the Tree of Knowledge has always been more effective in separating us from the Lord than the evil has. The goodness of man can be the most ugly manifestation of his pride and rebellion against God. The whole Tree of Knowledge must be torn from our soul by the roots.

Before Jesus could be revealed, the message of repentance had to be preached. This message alone could prepare the way for Him then, and this message alone can prepare the way for Him today. To repent means more than to have feelings of remorse because of sin and walk down some aisle; it means to *turn away* from sin. Sin is not just a few wrong things we have done; it is the nature of what we are — regardless of whether the guise is good or evil. In Christ, to repent means to renounce *all* that we are: our transgressions and that which we consider our righteousness. The Apostle Paul clearly articulated this in his letter to the church at Philippi.

> *Beware of dogs, beware of the evil workers, beware of the false circumcision; for we are the true circumcision, who worship in the Spirit of God and glory in Christ Jesus and **put no confidence in the flesh**, although I myself might have confidence even in the flesh.*

> *If anyone else has a mind to put confidence in the flesh, I far more: circumcised the eight day, of the nation of Israel, of the tribe of Benjamin, a Hebrew of Hebrews; as to the Law, a Pharisee; as to zeal, a persecutor of the church; as to the righteousness which is in the Law, **found blameless**.*

> *But whatever things were gain to me, those things I have counted as loss for the sake of Christ.*

> *More than that, I count all things to be loss in view of the surpassing value of knowing Christ Jesus my Lord, for whom I have suffered the loss of all things, and count them but rubbish in order that I may gain Christ, and may be found in Him, not having a righteousness of my own derived from the*

*Law, but that which is through faith in Christ, the righteous-
ness which comes from God on the basis of faith* (Phil. 3:2-9).

Paul's righteousness based on the Law brought Paul into direct
conflict with the Truth. He was a persecutor of true worshippers;
as is everyone who tries to live by the Law. Just as Cain could not
tolerate Abel, those who seek to stand by their own righteousness
find the presence of those who stand by faith in Jesus intolerable.
The righteousness of God, based completely on the atonement of
the cross, strips away facades and lays bare the pride of man. The
cross is the greatest threat to man's self-centeredness. As Paul
testified to the Philippians, to know Christ he had to give up
everything that he was. When he perceived the righteousness of
Jesus, he counted everything that he had so valued in life as
rubbish. This is an infallible testimony. Everything that we have
accomplished becomes less than worthless as we acknowledge who
He is and what He has accomplished. As the Queen of Sheba was
breathless before Solomon's splendor, we are far more so before
Jesus. And that which was the greatest threat to our self-will
becomes the source of peace and freedom so profound that it
challenges all human comprehension.

The Offerings

The spiritual roots of Cain and Abel are clearly discerned by the
offerings they brought to the Lord. Cain brought an offering of
grain, which in scripture typifies our own works. This is because of
the curse — the ground will only produce for man through toil and
sweat (Gen. 3:17-19). The grain was the fruit of Cain's sweat. Cain
thought that his works would be acceptable to the Lord as a
sacrifice. Descendants of the seed of Cain still feel this way. All who
have not had a revelation of the cross are continually trying to
balance the good and evil within themselves; believing that the good
they have done will outweigh the evil, thus making them acceptable
to God. Their defense is: "I'm a decent fellow"; or "I never hurt
anyone"; "I go to church"; "I give to the missions"; ad infinitum.
Benevolence offered as compensation for evil is an affront to the
cross of Jesus and will never be acceptable to the Father. *"All our*

righteous deeds are like a filthy garment" (Is. 64:6). Thus Cain's offering of works had to be rejected by the Lord.

Abel, however, offered a sacrifice of blood which was a type and prophecy of redemption through Jesus . . . *"Without shedding of blood there is no forgiveness"* (Heb. 9:22). This offering was received by the Lord and hence the conflict between two seeds which rages to this day. **The sacrifice is the point of conflict.**

The Lord's acceptance of Abel's offering so angered Cain that he slew his brother. The murderous nature of the seed of Cain is actually a defense mechanism rooted in insecurity. The self-righteousness of those seeking to be justified by their own works is very shaky, and deep inside they all know it. Because of this they are easily threatened by anyone who would challenge their delusion. We have a clear illustration of this through Saul of Tarsus before his conversion. By his testimony, according to the righteousness that was based on law he was found blameless (Phil. 3:6). When confronted by the truth that righteousness can only be found in Jesus, his very life's foundation was challenged. Enraged, he sought to destroy that which he accurately perceived to be the greatest threat to his righteousness. The cross of Jesus utterly destroys every self-righteous presumption. There is no greater intimidation to the knowledge of good and evil than the cross. The wrath generated in the seed of Cain by the cross and those who live by it is merely a desperate attempt at self-preservation. Understanding the matter from both sides, Paul confidently says: *"All who desire to live godly (righteous) in Christ Jesus will be persecuted"* (2 Tim. 3:12). Through the prophet Isaiah, the Lord made an astonishing statement:

> *Who is blind but My servant, or so deaf as My messenger whom I send? Who is so blind as he that is at peace with Me, or so blind as the servant of the Lord?* (Is. 42:19).

In a discourse with the Jews, the Lord Jesus expounded upon this revelation:

> *Jesus said to them, "If you were blind you would have no sin; but since you say, 'We see'; your sin remains"* (John 9:41).

Saul learned this on the road to Damascus. He had to be struck blind before he could truly see. Sooner or later, so does everyone that would come to know Jesus. Just as Saul had to become blind to the natural before he could see in the Spirit, so must the Cain in us all. If one thinks that he sees, then his sinful nature obviously remains. Only by the blinding Light can our sin be removed. Until we have been blinded, we will never truly see.

Abel

The scripture does not disclose whether Abel resisted Cain in their conflict, but if he was true to the nature of Jesus, he did not. Neither are we to resist personal injustices if we are faithful to Him, as He gave us instruction:

> You have heard that it was said, "An eye for an eye, and a tooth for a tooth." And if any one wants to sue you, and take your shirt, let him have your coat also. And whoever shall force you to go one mile, go with him two. Give to him who asks of you, and do not turn away form him who wants to borrow from you.

> You have heard that it was said, "You shall love your neighbor, and hate your enemy." But I say to you, love your enemies, and pray for those who persecute; in order that you may be sons of your Father who is in heaven; for He causes His sun to rise on the evil and the good, and sends rain on the righteous and the unrighteous.

> For if you love those who love you, what reward have you? Do not even the tax gatherers do the same? And if you greet your brothers only, what do you do more than others? Do not even the Gentiles do the same?

> Therefore you are to be perfect, as your heavenly Father is perfect (Matt. 5:38-48).

The Lord did not give us this commandment just for our own spiritual discipline. He gave it to us because there is a power in non-resistance to evil that crushes the serpent's head. It tears evil out by the roots: out of one's heart and his aggressor's. This commandment was given to forbid us from doing that by which evil is multiplied and perpetuated. If one attacks another, verbally or physically, evil is released. But if that evil is not able to affect its victim's patience, peace, or love that *"is not provoked, does not take into account a wrong suffered . . . bears all things, endures all things"* (1 Cor. 13:4-7), then the evil that was released is bound and defeated. Every blow that we are able to absorb without retaliation or resentment begins to consume the evil in the one who delivers it, as well as any that may be resident within us. *"If your enemy is hungry, feed him, and if he is thirsty, give him a drink; for in so doing you will heap burning coals (of conviction) upon his head"* (Rom. 12:20).

For the natural man it is very hard to perceive this principle. To him it seems that this only gives license to the evil; but there is a much higher spiritual principle involved. Satan cannot cast out Satan; anger cannot cast out anger; neither can resentment cast out wrath. If we react to evil, we are only multiplying the very demon we are seeking to cast out. But *"love covers a multitude of sins"* (1 Pet. 4:8). As Jesus explained, *"If I cast out demons by the Spirit of God, then the Kingdom of God has come upon you"* (Matt. 12:28). Jesus cast out Satan by allowing Satan to nail Him to the cross. To all the world, including His own disciples, it looked as if He were the one being cast out, not Satan. As paradoxical as it seems, the greatest injustice the world has ever known accomplished the greatest victory over evil. God's victories almost always seem like defeats to natural man.

The Lord allowed Paul to persecute His church and create much destruction in it for a time. To many of the persecuted, this was probably very hard to understand. But the Lord knew what this was to ultimately work for the vessel He had chosen to carry His name to "the Gentiles, kings and the sons of Israel". After Paul encountered Jesus on the road to Damascus, all the rage turned into humility and comprehension of the grace of God. The one who had been forgiven much would love much. After nearly two thousand years, the voice of this apostle is still one of the most powerful voices in the world. The church lamented greatly over the death of Stephen, but had they been able to foresee the ultimate effect his death would have on this young "Pharisee of Pharisees", they would have rejoiced.

'Truly, truly, I say to you, unless a grain of wheat falls into the earth and dies, it remains by itself alone; but if it dies it bears much fruit' (John 12:24).

Precious in the sight of the Lord is the death of His Godly ones (Ps. 116:15).

We may not see or understand the fruit ourselves, but whenever we lay down our lives or suffer persecution for the Lord's sake, there will be a triumph over evil and a glorious harvest from the seed that dies.

Abel's blood cried out from the ground (Gen. 4:10) as a prophecy that the blood of Jesus would cry out from the earth with the greatest message creation would ever hear. Jesus looked down from the cross at His tormentors without wrath or retaliation . . . but with mercy. He prayed, *"Father forgive them; they don't know what they're doing"* (Luke 23:34). These were not idle words — He meant it! He is not waiting until He comes again to get even. He forgave them. He knew they did not understand what they were doing. They lived in a darkness that could not be penetrated without the power of the sacrifice He had come to make for them, and was by their hands accomplishing. He did not come to condemn the world; it was already condemned. He came to save it. He has commissioned us with that same purpose. If it is to be accomplished through us, we too must lay down our lives.

To turn the other cheek to personal affront is never easy; it was not even easy for the Lord. Even the hope that we may be able to die to our self-will a little more will not give us the strength to endure. As the author of Hebrews declares, there is only one way for us to suffer injustice in the right spirit: by *"fixing our eyes on Jesus, the author and perfecter of faith, who for the joy set before Him, endured the cross, despising the shame, and has sat down at the right hand of the throne of God. For consider Him who endured such hostility by sinners against Himself, so that you may not grow weary and lose heart"* (Heb. 12:2-3). When Stephen fixed his eyes on Jesus, even the stones that were to kill him could not hold his attention. When he saw Jesus, he was filled with the love of God as he, too, begged forgiveness for his persecutors (Acts 7:54-60).

If we are to walk with Jesus, forgiving is not an option: it is a requirement. *"For if you forgive men for their transgression, your heavenly Father will also forgive you. But if you do not forgive men, then your Father will not forgive your transgression"* (Matt. 6:14-15).

The ability to suffer personal injustice without retaliation or resentment is an infallible sign that one has come to abide in Christ. *"For if we have become united with Him in the likeness of His death, certainly we shall also be in the likeness of His resurrection"* (Rom. 6:5). If we have truly been crucified with Christ, the greatest injustices will have no effect on us. If we have died with Christ, we are dead to the world. What could possibly affect a dead man? It is impossible for a dead man to retaliate. If we have died to the world, what can the world do to us?

> *Have this attitude in yourselves which was also in Christ Jesus, who although He existed in the form of God, He did not regard equality with God a thing to be grasped, but emptied Himself, taking the form of a bondservant, and being made in the likeness of men.*
>
> *And being found in appearance as a man, He humbled Himself by becoming obedient to the point of death, even death on a cross.*
>
> *Therefore also God highly exalted Him, and bestowed on Him the name which is above every name* (Phil. 2:5-9).

If the Lord Jesus, the Creator and King of the universe, would allow Himself to be humiliated for the sake of the ones that humiliated Him, how much more should we lay aside our rights for the sake of those whom He purchased with His own blood? The most exalted King of Glory became the most humble man, from His birth to His death, for us. How much more should we be willing to lay aside any claim to honor or position for His sake?

Under the Old Covenant, we were commanded to love our neighbors as ourselves. In Christ the calling is much higher. *"A new commandment I give to you, that you love one another even as I have loved you"* (John 13:34). Jesus did not just love us as He loved Himself; He loved us more than He loved His own life. That is how He has commanded us to love one another.

God's wrath will be poured out on this earth, and already has been in many ways; but we must understand His wrath. Jealousy is both a work of the flesh and a work of Satan (see Gal. 5:20 and James 3:14-15), yet it is testified many times in scripture that God is a jealous God. Is the Lord subject to the flesh or Satan? Of course not! The Lord's jealousy is not like man's jealousy. *"For My thoughts are not your thoughts, neither are your ways My ways', declares the Lord"* (Is. 55:8-9). Man's jealousy is carnal, self-centered, and often demonic. God's ways are higher than our ways. His jealousy is a pure jealousy, stimulated by a love for us, not self-preservation. Neither is His wrath like man's wrath. "God is love" and even His wrath is motivated by that which is His nature: LOVE. We often interpret His ways from the perspective of our ways, but His ways are infinitely higher. Viewing Him from our own perspective instead of through the Spirit has often caused man to distort the scriptures and purposes of God.

The apostle Paul exhorted us to *"Behold the kindness and the severity of God"* (Rom. 11:22). To our limited human minds, God's kindness and His severity seem to contradict one another. This has caused many to gravitate to one emphasis or the other. But if they are seen in the Spirit, there is complete harmony in His kindness and severity. His ways are higher than our ways and if we are to understand His ways we must be elevated so that we can see from His perspective. He cannot be understood correctly from the human perspective. To the world the cross is foolishness, but when the Lord opens our eyes, we see a glory that transcends human comprehension.

The Double-Mindedness of the Seed of Cain

There are certain characteristics being manifested with increasing frequency in men today which we would do well to understand.

None of these characteristics are new but their increase is significant. Like almost all human problems, their source can be traced to the Tree of Knowledge.

James wrote that the double-minded man is unstable in all his ways (James 1:18). This double-mindedness creates instability and is one of the most subtle, profound afflictions of the human race. Its manifestation is increasing greatly in both frequency and degree. It may well be the major contributing factor to the deep darkness and time of trouble that is prophesied to come upon the world in the last days.

What is double-mindedness? To be double-minded is to have more than one mind or personality. A common modern term for this problem is schizophrenia. We tend to think of schizophrenia in its most extreme forms: those in which drastic personality changes occur. (These extremes are often demonic in nature.) But there are degrees of double-mindedness found in all who have not been transformed from the carnal nature of fallen man by the renewing of their minds in Christ. If we tend to have one personality at home, another at the office or job, another at church, etc., these are symptoms of double-mindedness. It is a fruit of the Tree of Knowledge. Those who are trying to live by the knowledge of good and evil will have this problem. Men were not created to live with this knowledge, and it creates instability in us when we try to do so. We may think that such changes are normal, that we are just being flexible, but what is considered normal by the world's standards is not normal for the man God has re-created! There may be strong-willed people that can resist the changes in personality better than others, but given the right circumstances they too will bend and change. The only true stability that man can ever know is the Rock . . . Jesus.

Because of the self-centeredness incurred by the knowledge of good and evil and the compulsion to measure ourselves by it, as well as the fact that it is inherently "not good for man to be alone", one of the most dominating fears afflicting fallen man is the fear of rejection. This fear compels us to become the person we believe will be accepted or recognized, which will vary to some degree with each new group or situation. With each change we make to comply with external circumstances, there is a subtle erosion of the consistency and stability of our personality. Soon we are utterly confused as to who we really are and can be almost completely controlled by external circumstances.

With the infusion of certain philosophical and psychological theories recently, there has been an even greater erosion of human consistency in personality. In human transactions, from individuals to international foreign policy, the oscillations are becoming more and more pronounced. The sweeping changes in public opinion (as indicated by the political polls, for example) are astonishing in their swiftness. Our tendency to easily abandon one position for another is a telltale sign that we are fast losing our grip on just what we really believe in. There are powerful forces at work successfully undermining human stability. The future result will be an avalanche of debauchery the Bible calls the greatest time of trouble the world has ever seen.

Because our first parents tasted of the forbidden fruit (and whatever is sown must be reaped), every individual born on this earth has the inner knowledge of good and evil. To a degree, this knowledge has helped to keep man from utter chaos after our separation from God, but it is still the root of man's inner discord or depression. As the Lord explained to Cain: *"Why has your countenance fallen?* (or, Why are you depressed?) *If you do right, will not your countenance be lifted up? But if you do not do well, sin is crouching at the door, and its desire is for you. But you must master it"* (Gen. 4:6-7). Because of his inner knowledge of good and evil, Cain had to live by it. The Law is in every man. When man does what he knows is right, he feels good. When he doesn't, there is discord, regardless of how earnestly he tries to rationalize.

It is impossible for fallen man to wholly comply with the law in his heart. Sigmund Freud realized that the cause of man's depression was guilt, just as any honest seeker of truth will find if searching for the root of man's confusion. But he could not see past the Tree of Knowledge and supposed that the remedy was to be found in the very fruit that was causing the problem. Instead of teaching that the relief from guilt and resulting depression was to be found in doing what is right, he began to attack what he considered unrealistic morals and standards. This was done with great subtlety and effectiveness. Many of the trends toward lawlessness that are pervading the world today can be traced back to Freud's doctrines. Through them the door to the deepest, darkest corruption of the human heart was cracked open. As Margaret Thatcher, the Prime Minister of Great Britain, accurately discerned, "The veneer of civilization is very thin". Freud's theories escalated the stripping away of that very thin veneer. This was accurately foreseen by the psalmist several thousand years before our time:

'Why are the nations in an uproar, and the peoples devising a vain thing?'

The kings of the earth take their stand, and the rulers take counsel together against the Lord and against His Anointed:

Let us tear their fetters apart, and cast away their cords from us! (Ps. 2:1-3).

Freud accurately perceived that the Law is the source of man's depression, because no man can live up to its standards; and the resulting guilt brings depression. Paul articulated this in Romans chapter 7: *"For the good that I wish, I do not do; but I practice the very evil that I do not wish ..."* By this Paul concurred that the Law was good — but he was evil. He continued, *"For I know that nothing good dwells in me, that is, in my flesh, for the wishing is present in me, but the doing of good is not"* (Rom. 7:18). This conflict caused Paul to seek help in the only true solution to the dilemma — the Lord Jesus Himself. Freud turned to that which has been the cause of all the death and evil this planet has ever known — human reasoning. Instead of seeking the Lord's provision for our deliverance and from the Law and the body of death it manifests in us, Freud tried to rid man of the Law. Of course, this is impossible. Because we have eaten of the Tree of Knowledge, it is within us all. It will never go away. As the psalmist has discerned, attacking it will only bring about confusion among nations. The more we seek to ignore the Law, the more depressed and schizophrenic we will become. The philosophy of "removing the ancient boundaries" is in some form permeating every society of the world. The "deep darkness" that was prophesied to come over the world is being released (Is. 60:2).

The historian Will Durant observed that it is customs which keep men sane. Without grooves along which our minds can move with unconscious ease, we become perpetually hesitant and gripped with insecurity. Just as railroad tracks may restrict a train's freedom to move about, without them the train would go nowhere. Neither is man truly free to live in this world without the restrictions that God has placed upon him. The very thing that confines man is what sets him free to be what he was created to be. If a train tried to leave its tracks and take off across the countryside it would quickly become mired and unable to function. Since man decided to jump his "tracks", he has become increasingly mired in instability. Those who are choosing their own course to "freedom" are becoming the most bound of all. The tracks of good and evil are frustrating to man, but they are the only thing that keeps man stable until he comes to Christ.

During the fifties a great fear of communism began to permeate the West — especially the United States. Out of this era arose psychology for raising children that would supposedly bring out in them the character that would most vigorously resist tyranny. This philosophy glorified self-will and self-assertion. Psychologists, contrary to the wisdom of the scriptures, encouraged the restraint of parental discipline. They believed that discipline would hinder the free expression and independent development of the child's character. This generation that was projected to be uncompromising in their ideals actually became the student rebels, communists, and anarchists of the late sixties. They became the very enemies their parents were trying to bring them up to resist! The parents of this generation reaped only hatred and contempt. Why?

Again the law of flesh and spirit explains: *"If you feed the flesh you can only reap flesh and corruption"* (Gal. 6:8). Only by sowing to the Spirit can that which is Spirit be reaped. To feed self-will is to feed self-centeredness; and the self-centered are not capable of noble thought or deed. They are only concerned about their own needs and desires. These will actually be the most easily subverted by tyranny. Having the guidelines of authority eroded within themselves, they will seek security in that which is the most authoritarian. Any authority that appears weak or indecisive will be despised and attacked. All a tyrant has to do is promise security and the gratification of their flesh and he has won their allegiance.

The self-centered are not capable of attaining the higher principles of love, duty, justice, mercy, or even freedom — though they may vigorously preach these things. The self-centered may attach themselves to causes but the basic motivation of such attachment will be self-centered; i.e. personal recognition, rebellion, or the need to be identified with a strong social entity. The cause itself will be of secondary importance at best. Personal gratification toward noble or dramatic causes is merely an attempt to compensate for their excesses. The "me generation" has now come of age. The laying aside of personal ambition to become a true servant has become almost incomprehensible, yet this is precisely the course of the only true freedom we will ever know — becoming a servant of the Lord Jesus. Until He is the Center of our life, we cannot know true sanity or true freedom.

Man was created in the image of God and can only know his true identity when he is rightly related to God. Schizophrenia or multiple personalities, is perpetuated by a frustrated sense of identity. The schizophrenia of man is increasing as he moves further from the One in whose image he was made. Conversely, as we draw closer to Him, we come to know clearly who we really are. As we draw closer to Him, we will become the most consistent, decisive, stable people the world has ever known. External situations and social pressures will no longer bend us and shape us. The standard of the One who lives within us will be the Light by which we live. Jesus is the same yesterday, today, and forever. He never changes! Neither will the world be able to change us when our minds have been transformed so that we see with His eyes, hear with His ears and understand with His heart. The witness of the God who lives within us will become greater than all of the pressures that the world can possibly bring to bear. He is greater than the world!

Those who truly know their God are the most confident, humble and peaceful people on earth. As the Lord spoke through the prophet Isaiah: *"Behold, I am laying in Zion a stone, a tested stone, a costly cornerstone for the foundation, firmly placed. He who believes in it (Him) will not be disturbed"* (Is. 28:16). Jesus is the Cornerstone of the Creation. He is the only foundation for human life. When He is firmly placed in our lives, neither the whole world, nor all of the powers of evil, can disturb us. When we come to truly know our God, not just *about* Him, changes in our personality can no longer come from without; they can only come from within. His perfect love casts out all fear. In Him we no longer are moved by fear of rejection or fear of any other thing. In Him we do not live by fear, but faith.

The apostle John clearly and profoundly stated the difference between the two seeds:

> *No one who is born of God practices sin, because His seed abides in him; and he cannot sin, because he is born of God. By this the children of God and the children of the devil are obvious: anyone who does not practice righteousness is not of God, nor the one who does not love his brother.*

> *For this is the message which you have heard from the beginning, that we should love one another; not as Cain, who was of the evil one, and slew his brother. And for what did he slay him? Because his deeds were evil, and his brother's were righteous. Do not marvel, brethren, if the world hates you.*

> *We know that we have passed out of death into life, because we love the brethren. He who does not love abides in death. Everyone who hates his brother is a murderer; and you know that no murderer has eternal life abiding in him.*

> *We know love by this, that He laid down His life for us; and we ought to lay down our lives for the brethren. But whoever has the world's goods, and beholds his brother in need and closes his heart against him, how does the love of God abide in Him?*

> *Little children, let us not love with word or with tongue, but in deed and truth. We shall know by this that we are of the truth, and shall assure our heart before Him.* (1 John 3:9-19)

The distinguishing characteristics of those who are born of God are practicing righteousness and loving the brethren. This righteousness is not based on keeping the Law because *"by the works of the Law no flesh will be justified in His sight"* (Rom. 3:20) and *"Christ is the end of the Law for righteousness to everyone who believes"* (Rom. 10:4). He did not make an end of the Law by doing away with it, *but by fulfilling it* (Matt. 5:17). He accomplished that which no other human could. By this and the atonement which He made for our sins He has become our righteousness. Our "practice of righteousness" is to abide in Him. This faith is neither the act of a strong will, nor intellectual assessment and agreement with certain facts; it is the condition of heart. *"For with the heart man believes, resulting in righteousness"* (Rom. 10:10). Just believing with our minds will not accomplish this. True faith is of the heart, not the mind, and can only be accomplished by the new birth. Only the Spirit can beget that which is Spirit. The carnal nature of man (Cain) is at war with the Spirit. Only by the birthing of Christ within us can there be harmony with God. The strongest act of human will cannot accomplish this as the apostle testified in Romans 10:6-7:

> *But the righteousness based on faith speaks thus, "Do not say in your heart, 'who will ascend into heaven?' (that is, to bring Christ down), or 'Who will descend into the abyss?' (that is, to bring Christ up from the dead)."*

We cannot bring Christ down or call Him up. Salvation is beyond human attainment. Only Jesus can keep the Law of God's righteousness. If we focus on the Law, our sinful nature will consume us. If we focus our attention on Him, we will be changed into His image; the image we were originally created to bear. In Him there is no sin. If we abide in Him, there will be no sin in us.

When Jesus was asked by a scribe to name the great commandment, He answered: *"'You shall love the Lord your God with all your heart, and with all your soul, and with all your mind.' This is the great and foremost commandment. And the second is like it, 'You shall love your neighbor as yourself.'* **On these two commandments depend the whole Law and the Prophets"** (Matt. 22:37-40). If we could keep these two commandments we would keep the whole Law. If we loved the Lord with all our heart, we certainly would not commit idolatry; if we loved our neighbor, we would not murder, envy what is his, commit adultery with his wife, etc.

The whole law is fulfilled in these two commandments. Love is the fulfillment of the Law. Jesus replaced the negatives of the Law, the "do nots", with one simple positive — LOVE.

Which of us really loves the Lord with all our heart — or even our brother as ourself? *"The Lord has looked down from heaven upon the sons of men to see if there are any who understand, who seek after God. They have all turned aside; together they have become corrupt; there is no one who does good, not even one"* (Ps. 14:2-3). We would not even seek the Lord if He did not draw us. Which one of us is not convicted by I Corinthians 13? Only by abiding in Him can we practice righteousness. Jesus is our Righteousness. Jesus is the Love of God that has been shed abroad in our hearts.

We are transformed as we behold the glory of the Lord (2 Cor. 3:18). This is not accomplished by seeing Him and then looking back at ourselves comparatively (through the Tree of Knowledge). Our calling is not to be imitators of Christ, but to have Christ *formed* within us. When we begin to truly see His glory, we are too consumed with the wonder of Him to be aware of, or even interested in, ourselves and what we may have attained to. When the twenty-four elders in Revelation saw the Lamb, they cast their crowns at His feet. Who could glory in His presence? When we start trying to define our position in Christ, we begin to lose that position. *He is* the finished work of God. *He is* the finished work of the Church. We are growing up into Him. The issue is not what we are, but what He is. He is the Tree of Life. If we are partaking of Him, we will live forever.

3

Babylon

The building of the Tower of Babel is one of the more lucid revelations of the substance and motivation of the carnal nature of man. In one sentence, the men of Babel sum up that which is the innervation of the earthly-minded:

> *Come let us build for ourselves a city and a tower whose top will reach into heaven, and let us make a name for ourselves; lest we be scattered abroad over the face of the whole earth* (Gen. 11:4).

The Lord created us for His pleasure for fellowship and service. The only true fulfillment we will ever know is found in serving Him, yet the fruit of the Tree of Knowledge has turned us almost completely inward. Now man's only intent is to serve himself, an endeavor that inevitably results in great frustration.

As ludicrous as the attempt to build a tower to heaven may seem, men have never stopped trying to complete it. History is a long train of unfinished towers — the ruins of man's attempt to make a name for himself and unite around the various towers. Grievously, Christians have seemed just as determined to build these towers to heaven. Regardless of how piously we attach the Lord's name to our works, everything motivated by selfish ambition will come to the same end as the original tower — confusion and scattering. As James clearly explained. *"Selfish ambition is earthly, natural, demonic. For where jealously and selfish ambition exist, there is disorder (confusion) and every evil thing"* (James 3:15-16).

The Lord looked down on the men of Babel and determined that the scattering of their languages was the best solution to their folly. Babel means "confusion". The Lord looked at what many believed to be the Christian church in the Middle Ages and saw the same folly. Much of the visible church is another form of the original tower . . . an attempt by men to reach heaven by their own works. So the Lord scattered its languages too; now there are over 1800 different languages or denominations. Regardless of how good their works may seem, every work that is an attempt to gather men around anything but the Lord Jesus Himself has its origin in the carnal nature of man. It doesn't matter if it's a building, project, evangelical outreach, or a great spiritual truth — if it is an attempt to gather men, confusion will result. Jesus alone can gather men together. Certainly there is nothing wrong with projects, outreaches, or true spiritual doctrine; but if these become our focal point, the Lord will ultimately have to have to separate us from them for our own good.

One can understand all Christian doctrine accurately and yet not be a Christian. Being a Christian is not just understanding certain doctrines and spiritual principles — it is having one's life in Jesus. If the truth leads us to life in Jesus, it has accomplished its purpose. But if the truth becomes the focal point, it kills . . . it is the knowledge of good and evil. Most denominations originated with a genuine move of the Spirit that imparted truth to the Church — a truth that would lead the Church closer to Jesus. Many benefitted with a more intimate walk with Him. Others never saw beyond the truth and began to build their towers, which resulted in many denominations.

Babylon is not just a physical reality; Babylon is in the heart. There are many "non-denominational" churches that are as sectarian as any denominational church. Likewise, there are some denominational churches in which Jesus is truly the head and there seems to be little or no sectarian spirit. There are some who have truth without life; and there are some who have life in Jesus and yet may not understand all doctrine correctly. As Thomas a'Kempis reflected, "I would rather feel contrition than know the definition thereof . . . What does it avail a man to be able to discourse profoundly concerning the Trinity if he is void of humility and thereby displeasing to Trinity?" Fleeing from physical Babylon is not just leaving a denomination or sect; it is the removal of all barriers that separate us from the Lord and our brothers that we might freely love and freely serve. As the apostle exhorted, *"From now on we recognize no man* (or church?) *according to the flesh* (externals)" (2 Cor. 5:16).

Truth is important. There are basic truths that we must have in proper order if we are to remain on the path that leads to life. But there are many doctrines not in this category that believers through the ages have separated over. Christians, disciples of Jesus that He said would be recognized by their love, have demonstrated the uncanny ability to agree on 98% of their doctrines and separate from one another over the 2% they disagree on. Requisite agreement on every little detail is rooted in insecurity. The insecurity of the leadership of the Body of Christ has been the source of as much division within the Church as any other single factor. The insecure are threatened by even the slightest deviation from their own beliefs and tend to greatly overreact to such deviations. Polarizations can become bitter and irreconcilable over petty differences. This is a symptom that one's authority is not rooted in Christ. Overreacting to challenges is evidence that one is in fact building for himself. If one is rooted and abiding in Christ, he will not be intimidated by even the most severe challenges. He understands the Lord's supreme authority and power.

Nothing is impossible with God. It would be a small thing for Him to have us all believing the same way about everything. Presently He has a good reason for not doing this. We must first understand that our unity is not based on doctrines. Such unity is superficial at best. We must understand that our unity can only be found in Jesus. To focus our attention on Him and learn to love and cover one another is far more important than agreeing on all doctrines. Having like doctrines is not a basis for unity . . . it is a basis for division! When the Lord becomes our focal point, we will see doctrines and everything else from the same perspective.

We are exhorted to *"examine everything carefully; hold fast to that which is good"* (1 Thes. 5:21). We are foolish if we do not examine everything carefully by the Word and the Spirit. Nevertheless, we are just as foolish if we examine teaching in the wrong spirit. The exhortation is to hold fast to that which is good; not that which is bad. Examination is not for the purpose of looking for what is wrong — but what is right. When we examine with the intent of challenging, it frequently distorts what we are actually hearing. Some seem to have more faith in the devil to deceive them than they do in the Holy Spirit to lead them into all truth. Again, this is manifestation of our insecurity and has led to much division and misunderstanding in the Body of Christ. There are times when challenge or confrontation is necessary to bring correction. The New Testament epistles are largely a result of the apostles and elders doing just that. But understand that the Lord's correction is healing and restorative. Our abrasiveness can make healing and restoration much more difficult for a person that is in error.

Almost every great truth imparted to the Church has been carried to extremes by those who first received it. As a result the rest of the Church embraced the opposite extreme in overreaction. Frequently the overreactions have caused as much harm as the extremes to which the doctrine may have originally been carried. The truth that leads to life is usually found somewhere between the extremes. Those who are of either extreme position usually consider the true path a compromise. Historically the majority of the Body of Christ has simply shied away from the whole issue because of the confusion, which is also a mistake. The wise "examine everything carefully; holding fast to that which is good". If we are living our lives more before men than before the Lord, we will easily be swayed by the pressure and confusion. If we are led by the Spirit, as all true sons of God are (Rom. 8:14), then He will faithfully lead us into all truth.

We must judge the root of a work before we devote ourselves to it, regardless of how "scriptural" it may seem. The Lord never said that we would know men, or their works, by how scriptural they are. Their true nature can only be known by their fruit. Is the fruit from the Tree of Life, or the Tree of Knowledge? It does not matter how much "good" a work seems to do . . . the Tree of Knowledge is rooted just as much in good as it is in evil. If the fruit is not Jesus, it is not life.

The overwhelming majority of doctrinal errors are usually overemphasis of isolated scriptures. That is why Paul exhorted Timothy to *"rightly divide the word of truth"* (2 Tim. 2:15). Psalm 119:160 states, *"The sum of Thy word is truth"*. To rightly divide the scriptures we must see the whole word of God. Many things in the written word purposely seem contradictory. Because of this, we often gravitate toward one position or the other, overlooking what we do not understand, or worse, rationalizing our preference. This has led to polarizations over almost every Christian doctrine. We are often distracted from the River of Life by the little tributaries. Only when we are able to see the sum of all truth are we able to accurately understand any single part of it. **Jesus is the sum of all spiritual truth.** All things will be summed up in Jesus (Eph. 1:10). As we behold Him, all of the seemingly disconnected parts come together in breathtaking harmony.

Walking in truth is not just understanding everything accurately, it is abiding in Him who is the Truth. Growing spiritually is not just growing in knowledge but *"growing up into Him"* (Eph. 4:15). Deception is not just misunderstanding a doctrine; it is not being in His will. The Body of Christ is not made of many warring fragments; it is a living, functioning organism made up of different parts that together make a whole. The true Body of Christ is not, and never was, divided. *"Since there is one bread, we who are many are ONE BODY: for we all partake of the one bread"* (1 Cor. 10:17).

The Pride of the Seed of Cain

The building of the Tower of Babel is a profound illustration of the pride of the seed of Cain. The men of Babel actually believed that they could reach heaven by their own efforts. "Let us build ... let us make". This is an echo of the serpent's temptation of Eve — that she could become like God without God. Since the success of that temptation, Satan has been able to keep man devoted to this folly. Man has fearfully bowed his knee to many idols, but he has always had one god . . . himself. The serpent tempted man to go his way and since that day man has been utterly determined to do just that. This inclination to independence brought death into the world and has been its perpetuating force. That is a reflection of Satan's own inclination. The prophet Isaiah articulated that which was the boast of the "king of Babylon", a personification of Satan:

"I WILL ascend to heaven. I WILL raise my throne above the stars of GOD. I WILL sit on the mount of the assembly. I

*WILL ascend above the heights of the clouds. **I will make
myself like the most high***" (Is. 14:13-14).

This attitude of being able to individually attain self-perfection
is obvious in every religion and philosophy in the world except true
Christianity. The attitude of making one's self into what one should
be is so pervasive that even the most sincere and devoted Christian
may not be aware of how much this spirit rules his own life. Some
of us have been so deceived that we not only think that we can
make ourselves what we should be, but others as well! Let us
understand, the Lord *wants* us to ascend to heaven; He *wants* us to
sit on the mount of the assembly; He *wants* us to be raised above
the heights of the clouds, **and He wants us to be like Him** (have His
nature). But only He can accomplish this for us (which He has
done through His Son). It has been a primary strategy of Satan
through the ages to tempt man to grasp for himself what the Lord
ultimately intends to give us anyway. The victory of Jesus over
Satan was accomplished when *"He did not consider equality with God
a thing to be grasped"* (Phil. 2:6), but humbled Himself instead,
waiting for the Father to exalt Him at the proper time.

The Antithesis to Babylon

At Babel the Lord scattered man's languages so that they could
no longer understand each other and continue building the tower
of futility. On the Day of Pentecost, when the Lord first baptized
men in His Holy Spirit, He gave His people a gift that was to be a
sign to the world that His Church was to be the antithesis to the
Tower of Babel. At Babel, man's languages were confused; at
Pentecost, all men could understand a common language. What
they heard testified by that common language were the *"wonderful
works of God"* (Acts 2:11), which was in direct contrast to the futile
works of man typified by the tower.

Of course, the gift through which men heard the testimony of
God's works was the gift of tongues. It is not strange that this gift
would be the most controversial of the gifts of the Spirit. To the
natural man, its purpose and practical use is incomprehensible. To
the spiritual man, it is the language of God that penetrates all

facades to touch the inner man. The language of the Spirit testifies of the Language of God in whom all men will one day be found together in perfect unity.

The Lord's judgement upon Babylon was not condemnation. God wants us understand that only through Jesus can we truly be united. No amount of ecumenical zeal or good intentions can bring men together. Our oneness can only be of Him and in Him. When He is truly lifted up He will draw all men to Himself. He is the only common denominator through which there can be true communication and interrelations among men and, most importantly, between men and their Creator. Only through Him can we truly understand ourselves, others, and the Father.

Before His crucifixion the Lord prayed for His church *"that they may all be one; even as Thou Father, art in Me, and I in Thee, that they may also be in Us; that the world may believe that Thou didst send Me"* (John 17:21). The church that the world tried to build is degenerating into increasing confusion, just as its predecessor at Babel. The church that the Lord is building will one day astonish the world with its unity. It will be a unity that transcends covenants and agreements; it will be a unity that could only come through a *union* with the One who holds all things together by the word of His power. This unity will not come by seeking unity; it can only come by seeking Him. We may be completely oblivious to it, because our attention will not be on ourselves but on Him. Unity for its own sake can be a false god. If we are seeking Him, unity will come.

When Jesus was asked by the people, *"What shall we do that we may work the works of God?"* His reply was to the point: *"This is the work of God that you believe in Him whom He has sent"* (John 6:28-29). **Jesus is the finished work of God.** He was the beginning of the work of God and He is the end, the Alpha and Omega. Understanding this, the apostle had a single-minded purpose to his ministry: *"And we proclaim Him, admonishing every man and teaching every man with all wisdom, that we may present every man complete in Christ. And for this purpose I labor striving according to His power, which mightily works within me"* (Col. 1:28-29). Jesus is the work of God. Everything that God is doing is found in Christ, just as the ultimate end of all things will be summed up in Him (Eph. 1:10).

Jesus is called the *"Beginning of the creation of God"* (Rev. 3:14). Everything that the Father loved and esteemed He brought forth in His Son. He is the delight of the Father and the exact representation of His nature. The Father loves the Son above all and the Son loves the Father above all. The Holy Spirit is the personification and power of this love. In everything that was created, the Father was looking for His Son. He is looking for His Son in us.

> *For by Him all things were created, both in the heavens and on earth, visible and invisible, whether thrones or dominions or rulers or authorities — **all things have been created by Him and for Him.***
>
> *And He is before all things, and **in Him all things hold together.***
>
> *He is also the head of the body, the church; and He is the beginning, the first-born from the dead; **so that He Himself might come to have first place in EVERYTHING.***
>
> *For it was the Father's good pleasure for all the fullness to dwell in Him.*
>
> *and through Him to reconcile all things to Himself, having made peace through the blood of His cross; through Him I say, whether things on earth or things in heaven* (Col. 1:16-20).

The labor of the apostles was not devoted to persuading the Church to comply with certain doctrines, but that Christ would **be formed** in the Church. To this Paul testified to the Galatians: *"My children, with whom I am again in labor until **Christ is formed in you**"* (Gal. 4:19). This is the purpose of all true ministry — that Christ is formed. Jesus is the finished work. Our goal is not formation, but TRANSFORMATION!

> *He made known to us the mystery of His will, according to His kind intention which He purposed in Him with a view to an administration suitable to the fullness of times, that is, **the summing up of all things in Christ,** things in heaven and things upon the earth, in Him* (Eph. 1:9-10).

"That which is born of flesh is flesh; and that which is born of the Spirit is Spirit" (John 3:6). Only the Spirit of God can bring forth Christ. The absolute best human intentions can only bring forth that which is flesh. The best that man can offer is still rooted in The Tree of Knowledge. Because of this Paul explained to the men of Athens: *"He (God) is not served by human hands"* (Acts 17:25) Jesus testified: *"An hour is coming, and now is, when the true worshippers shall worship the Father in Spirit and truth; for such people the Father seeks to be His worshippers. God is Spirit; and those who worship Him must worship Him in Spirit and truth"* (John 4:23-24). We will be worshippers to the degree that we are open to His Spirit to move through us.

Many that are born again and baptized in the Holy Spirit reflect no change in their approach to life. Though external behavior patterns may have changed, they continue to be primarily cognizant of the material realm. This may be due to the way they relate to Jesus. There is a tendency to continue relating to Him as *"the MAN from Galilee"*. Jesus is not a man. He was and is Spirit. He took the **form** of a servant and became a man for a brief time. The Scripture testifies that we are changed by the way we behold His glory (2 Cor. 3:18). Beholding Him as a natural man does little to change us into the new creation He has called us to be. The Lord testified to Caiaphas: *"Hereafter* (or "from now on") *you shall see the Son of Man sitting at the right hand of power and coming on the clouds of heaven"* (Matt. 26:64). He was saying after His crucifixion we would see Him in the power of His resurrection. When we begin to see Him in this light, we profoundly understand why "He is not served by human hands".

After His resurrection, the disciples even had trouble recognizing Him. They were more dependent on His physical appearance than His spiritual nature. Understanding this, He told them before His crucifixion it was expedient that He go away so His Spirit could be sent (John 16:7). Men have historically had the tendency to know Him after the flesh rather than the Spirit. Jesus cannot be reduced to a natural-sense perception! It was because of the tendency that He gave the second commandment: *"Thou shalt make no graven image of the Lord thy God"*. Anything that man could make to represent Him would inevitably be a gross misrepresentation. We could never accurately perceive Him with our natural eyes

or natural minds. He can only be perceived through the Spirit.
The Lord has continued to say to His church just what He said to
Philip: *"Have I been with you so long and yet you have not come to
know Me?"* (John 14:9).

On the Mount of Transfiguration we have a vivid example of an
encounter between the glorified Christ and men that have not yet
been transformed from the carnal nature of Cain. Matthew 17:1-8
reads:

> *Jesus took with Him Peter and James and John his brother and
> brought them up to a high mountain by themselves.*

> *And He was transfigured before them; and His face shown like
> the sun, and His garments became as white as light.*

> *And, behold, Moses and Elijah appeared to them talking to
> Him.*

> *And Peter answered and said to Jesus, "Lord it is good for us
> to be here; if You wish I WILL make three tabernacles here,
> one for You, and one for Moses, and one for Elijah".*

> *While he was still speaking, behold, a bright cloud, overshad-
> owed them; and behold a voice out of the cloud, saying, "This
> is My beloved Son, hear Him!"*

> *And when the disciples heard this, they fell on their faces and
> were much afraid.*

> *And Jesus came to them and touched them and said, "Arise,
> and do not be afraid".*

> *And lifting up their eyes, they saw no one except Jesus Himself
> alone.*

After observing Jesus' magnificent transfiguration, *"Peter
answered!"* No one was even addressing Peter! And what came out
of his mouth? *"It is good for us to be here . . . I WILL."* Sound
familiar? True, it was good for them to be there . . . but not for

Peter's reasons. It was good for them to glimpse the glory of their Lord. It was good for them to heed the Father's rebuke: *"Hear Him"*. They were not there to hear Moses (a type of the Law), or Elijah (a type of the Church) but to hear Jesus! After they heard the command it is recorded: *"Lifting up their eyes, they saw no one, except Jesus Himself alone"*. This was the purpose for which they had been brought to the mountain — their vision was to be focused on Him alone. We also must see Him transformed from "the Man of Galilee" into the glorified Son. We must hear in the depths of our beings the voice that exhorts us to forget about what *we* can build and *"Hear HIM"*.

4

Abraham

Abraham offers a sharp contrast to the men of Babel. He was of a different spirit. His trust was not in himself, but in the Lord. As the men of Babel strove to build for themselves an eternal, earthly city, Abraham proved time after time his willingness to give up everything on earth to seek a heavenly city. He left Ur of the Chaldees, his father's house and family; he later drove out his firstborn son Ishmael; he even proved willing to sacrifice his promised son Isaac. Instead of striving to build for himself, he continually released everything to the Lord, trusting Him to accomplish all that concerned him. Because of his faith, the Lord accomplished for Abraham all that the men of Babel had vainly sought — a name that would be esteemed for all generations a city that would last forever.

Because natural men cannot conceptualize the things that are eternal, they often think if they can somehow attain renown among men they will not utterly perish. When we begin to perceive the Eternal One, to be remembered by men has little significance; to be known by the Lord is enough. As we perceive the glory of the Lord, all earthly cities and achievements of men begin to lose their shine. Human claim to honor or position appears ludicrous. As we draw near to Him, we will lose interest in any city which man can build — the city which God has built will have all our attention.

Abraham was able to believe God because he was a man of spiritual vision; he was able to "look" at things which the natural eye cannot see. Being a spiritual man he understood that *"the things which are seen are temporal, the things which are not seen are eternal"* (2 Cor. 4:18). When the Lord opens the "eyes of our hearts" to the eternal realm, our vision ceases to be limited by space and time; the future becomes as real as the present. Abraham was able to offer Isaac as a sacrifice because he had looked ahead to the sacrifice of Jesus as the Lord Himself confirmed: *"Your father Abraham rejoiced to see My day; and he saw it and was glad"* (John 8:56). Abraham had prophetically foreseen the crucifixion and resurrection of Jesus, and he understood that his son Isaac was a type of the coming Messiah." Comprehending this, he made Isaac carry the wood for his own sacrifice just as Jesus was to carry His own cross. Abraham knew that just as Jesus was to be raised, so would his own son. (See Heb. 11:19.)

True faith is not a recipe that can be learned by rote. It is neither a feeling nor an intellectual assessment nor an agreement with certain principles. True faith can only come with spiritual vision. The apostle explained that "the eyes of our hearts" must be opened (Eph. 1:18), for *"with the heart man believes"* (Rom. 10:10). True faith is simply the recognition of the One in whom we believe. True faith is knowing Jesus; it is the ability to see Him in the power of His resurrection, as Abraham was able to do even before He came. Faith is not just believing the words of the Lord, but believing the Word Himself.

There are spiritual principles that work in the spiritual realm just as there are natural laws that work in the natural realm. These spiritual principles will work for anyone that uses them. In fact Satan's power is completely dependent upon God-ordained principles; he merely bends them for his own purposes. One can have this "faith" in the principles and do mighty works completely apart from God. By this faith many commercial faith healers and spiritualists perform their lying wonders. There are even sincere Christians that have wandered from the true faith to a faith that is reduced to principles and laws that are learned . . . and do work. But the difference between true faith and counterfeit is easily discerned by its fruit. The true faith is in God; the other is merely faith in one's faith, or principles and laws. True faith comes by seeing the Lord and its fruit will be love and humility. The fruit of counterfeit faith will always be pride. Such feeds the lusts of man and not his spirit. Many of the doctrines that are called "faith" today are the result of dangerous grasping by those who are still earthly-minded. In these cases, the thrust of the teaching will place a great deal of emphasis on earthly blessing and attainment: *"For those who are according to the flesh set their minds on the things of the flesh, but those who are according to the Spirit, the things of the Spirit"* (Rom. 8:5). Paul pointedly warned Timothy of the very thing that is today still making shipwreck of many Christians' spiritual lives:

> *Godliness actually is a means of great gain, when accompanied by contentment.*
>
> *For we have brought nothing into the world, so we cannot take anything out of it either.*
>
> *And if we have food and covering, with these we shall be content.*
>
> *But those who want to get rich fall into temptation and a snare and many foolish and harmful desires which plunge men into ruin and destruction.*
>
> *For the love of money is a root of all sorts of evil, and some by longing for it have wandered away from the faith, and pierced themselves with many a pang.*
>
> *But flee from these things, you man of God; and pursue righteousness, godliness, faith, love, perseverance and gentleness.*
>
> *Fight the good fight of faith; take hold of eternal life* (1 Tim. 6:6-12).

To be rich or poor in the things of the world has nothing to do with our spirituality or our degree of faith. Some think it more spiritual to be poor and may be squandering foolishly, yet it is not God's will for them. Some just as foolishly devote themselves to material wealth. True faith is demonstrated by having peace in whatever circumstances the Lord has us in, as Paul further testified:

> *I have learned to be content in whatever circumstances I am.*

> *I know how to get along with humble means, and I also know how to live in prosperity; in any and every circumstance I have learned the secret of being filled and going hungry, both of having abundance and suffering need* (Phil. 4:11-12).

Was Paul lacking in faith when he went hungry? When he suffered need? By his own testimony, his contentment in those circumstances *was faith*. But just as we must learn contentment in times of need, we must also learn how to live in prosperity and keep a level head. If we cannot be responsible with the earth's riches, we certainly will not be capable of managing heavenly riches. But if we, like Paul, have perceived the spiritual riches in Christ, all the world's riches will be of little consequence. This faith cannot be faked or conjured by a repetitious quoting of scripture. It can only come from "seeing Him who is unseen", as Moses did when he turned down all the riches of Egypt to follow Him.

The promises of God are not given so that we can *do* and *have*, but so that we can *be* (found in Him). That is why the promises of God are not made to us as individuals but to Jesus, as the apostle explains: *"for as many as may be the promises of God, in Him they are yes"* (2 Cor. 1:20). Paul further clarified this to the Galatians: *"Now the promises were spoken to Abraham and to his seed,* (He does not say, 'And to his seeds', referring to many, but rather to one: 'And to your seed') *that is Christ"* (Gal. 3:16). He reiterated this again in his letter to the Ephesians: *"I pray that the eyes of your heart may be enlightened, so that you may know what is the hope of His calling, what are the riches of the glory of His inheritance in the saints, and what is the surpassing greatness of His power toward us who believe. These are in accordance with the working of the strength of His might"* (Eph. 1:18-19).

When Satan tempted Jesus in the wilderness, he tried to entice Him to claim the promises of God for selfish reasons. He is still using the same temptation today to cause God's people to stumble. The promises of God are glorious beyond comprehension. However, none of the promises were meant to be taken independently of Jesus. It is the Lord Himself who is our inheritance. The promises were given "in Him" as they are all given for His glory and His purposes. They were given in Him so all of our attention would be on Him — not ourselves. We do not perform great miracles by believing who we are in Christ, but by believing in Him. *"Truly, truly, I say to you, he who believes in Me, the works that I do shall he do also; and greater works than these shall he do; because I go to the Father"* (John 14:12).

In the sixth chapter of John, a great separation takes place among the people who were following Jesus. In verse 2 we see a great multitude following Him *because* they were seeing the signs that He was performing. Others were following Him because of the loaves that He multiplied and fed to them (verse 26). Some followed Him for miracles, others because of His provision for their needs. Men have changed little. If one is intent on having great crowds follow their ministry, the performing of miracles or the preaching of God's provision will always bring out the multitudes. But Jesus knew that these motives were superficial and would have to be changed. The line had to be drawn — the wheat and chaff separated. He challenged them: *"Do not work for the food which perishes, but for the food which endures to eternal life, which the Son of man shall give you, for on Him the Father, even God has set His seal"* (verse 27). They did not understand what He was saying: *"They therefore said to Him, 'What shall we do, that we may work the works of God?'"* (verse 28). The Lord again tried to correct their motives: *"This is the work of God, that you believe in Him whom He has sent"* (verse 29). The multitude's reply to this was to ask for a sign and manna from heaven. The Lord's answer was that He was the Bread from heaven and unless they ate His flesh and drank His blood, they would not have life. In one of the saddest testimonies of motivation, the apostle records: *"As a result of this many of His disciples withdrew, and were not walking with Him anymore"* (verse 66).

When it was narrowed down to those who were following Him for who He was and not for what He could do, there were not many left. Those who withdrew were not just stragglers picked up by the excitement of the crowd — they were *disciples*. If the Lord were to make this same challenge today, how many would be left? As Peter supposed he would never deny Him, it is hard for us to believe that we would ever leave Him. But we are no different. When that challenge comes (and it will), from a multitude there will be only a handful left.

At this point the ministry of Jesus dramatically changed. Until that time He devoted most of His attention to the multitudes; after this His efforts were directed almost entirely to His disciples. Before this incident He had performed miracles so the people would believe in Him; from this point on He only performed miracles for those who did believe in Him.

Of course the Lord desires to bless His people. However, when we desire the blessings and gifts more than Him, serious problems result. Self-centeredness is a poison that is killing us. When we receive His blessings in a way that perpetuates our egocentricity, in His mercy He often stops the blessings. The entire history of ancient Israel is a continuous cycle of deliverance, blessing, complacency, idolatry, bondage, oppression, humility and seeking the Lord . . . then the cycle begins anew. They never did get the message. Will we?

The Lord called the Church to be His bride. How would any husband feel if he found out that his wife only married him for his wealth and if the expensive gifts stopped she would leave him? Where would the joy be if the only time his wife communicated with him was when she wanted something? It would be a lifeless marriage. Is there life in our union with the Lord?

If the Lord had more of our attention, and the blessings less, we would probably be walking in more blessing. The promise is that if we seek *first* His kingdom everything else will be added to us (Matt. 6:33). Of course He wants us to appreciate our inheritance, but compared to him, all the treasures are insignificant! When we begin to really see Him, we will cast our crowns at His feet.

Faith and Patience

Hebrews 6:12 exhorts us to *"be imitators of those who through faith and patience inherit the promises"*. Faith has become a very popular subject in the body of Christ in the last few years; but the other necessary ingredient, patience, is almost entirely overlooked. The result has been tragic.

True faith cannot be separated from patience. Patience is the demonstration of true faith, as Abraham proved by his example. Not only were he and Sarah very old when the promise of a son was given, but the Lord required them to wait many more years until He fulfilled the promise. Instead of being discouraged by the passing of time, their faith in the Lord grew stronger, and when God did fulfill His promise, there was no doubt that *He* had done it.

In hope against hope he believed, in order that he might become the father of many nations.

And without becoming weak in faith he contemplated his own body, now as good as dead since he was about a hundred years old, and the deadness of Sarah's womb;

yet, with respect to the promise of God, he did not waver in unbelief, but grew strong in faith, giving glory to God (Rom. 4:18-20).

Time is an unfailing test of faith. If our faith is the true faith of God, it will grow stronger, regardless of the circumstances that appear to make fulfillment remote. If it is not true faith, time will erode it. God has ordained that it would take faith *and* patience to inherit His promises. Time will remove that which is not true and strengthen that which is true.

The Lord compared faith to a mustard seed. This is a very tiny seed and yet it can grow to great planthood and bear fruit. But lest we misunderstand, the seed is *not* the fruit. The seed must be planted, watered and cultivated to become a healthy plant and only then can it bear fruit. It is the same with faith. That which we interpret as faith is often the seed planted within us to be watered and cultivated.

The true faith of God *can* move mountains, raise the dead and heal the sick. There is such a maturity and submission in God required just to *perceive* real faith that I think the universe and God's plan are quite safe from the foolish interference of immature (though well-meaning) Christians. It is wonderful and exciting when the Lord performs instantaneous miracles, but those that take a little longer are no less miracles. It amazed the disciples when Jesus turned the water into wine, but the Lord turns water into wine today — He just takes a little longer. It must have been wondrous to see the fig tree wither after the Lord cursed it, but there has never been a tree that withered unless the Lord cursed it; neither has a sickness ever been cured except by His hand. True faith sees His hand in everything, regardless of the amount of time He takes, or the manner in which He does His work. As Elizabeth Browning once remarked, "Earth is crammed with heaven. Every bush is aflame with the fire of God, but only those who see take off their shoes. The rest just pick the berries". True faith is seeing Him and abiding in Him. There are no cheap substitutes or easy formulas. If we are seeking true faith, like Abraham we must allow ourselves to be carried well beyond the limits of human ability.

Because many ministries have misunderstood the correlation between faith and patience, there has been a tendency for them to extend their borders beyond what they were called to do. There is a mentality resulting from unbalanced faith teaching that infers if one is not continually expanding they are not walking in faith. Because of this ministry, programs and newsletters are increasingly dominated by desperate appeals for money; their testimony to God's faithfulness being that if they do not hear from **us** soon they will be forced to go off the air. This has caused much grief and humiliation to the whole Body of Christ. The Lord promised that His seed would not beg for bread (Ps. 37:25). When the Lord ordains a work, there will be no lack of provision to accomplish it. When Moses asked the people for a contribution to construct the tabernacle, he had to restrain the people because they brought too much! When a ministry has to beg, plead or threaten the body of Christ for its support, something is wrong.

The scriptural examples of how the Lord prepares his servants are in stark contrast to trends today. After Joseph's dream, it seemed that only the opposite of what had been foretold would ever come true in his life. After he saw the sun and moon and stars bowing down to him, **he** became a **slave**! After finally finding favor with his master, he is sent to the dungeon! According to popular teaching today, he was not walking in enough faith. In reality great faith was nourished mightily in him with each new trial. He knew that to be used for the Lord's purposes, humility came before exaltation: *"Therefore, humble yourselves under the mighty hand of God, that He may exalt you **at the proper time**"* (1 Pet. 5:6).

Between the place we receive the promise and the promised land is a wilderness that is the exact opposite of what we've been promised. Israel was promised a land flowing with milk and honey but in their initial wanderings there was not even water! In that place they were to learn profoundly the fruit of their own strivings. When they did finally enter the promised land they were given homes which they did not build, cisterns which they did not dig, and vineyards which they did not plant (Deut. 6:10-11). Certainly there were great battles to be fought in that land, but the provision was from God. It has been the "I will" of man that has kept him at enmity with the purposes of God. We will never possess His promises until the "I will" is replaced with "He will", because "human hands cannot serve Him". The best human intentions and strivings to build for Him will not serve His purposes.

Ishmael

Ishmael was the result of Abraham's lapse of patience in waiting for the Lord. After several years of waiting for a son, he began to follow his own reasoning instead of the leading of the Spirit. His wife suggested He lie with her maiden for his son. Abraham made a terrible mistake by not seeking the Lord about it; he went in to Hagar and she conceived and gave birth to Ishmael. As the apostle Paul later testifies, this child was born after the flesh, not after the Spirit (Gal. 4:23). Ishmael was of the seed of Cain.

The effect of Abraham's lack of patience has been a devastating historical reality. Just as there has been enmity between the Arabs (Ishmael's descendants) and the Jews (Isaac's descendants) since that time, there will always be enmity between that which is born of the flesh and the true seed of God. By the time Isaac was weaned, Ishmael was already mocking him (Gen. 21:9). Finally Abraham drove Ishmael out of his house and disallowed his inheritance. A tree can only bear fruit after its own kind. That which is sown in the flesh must be reaped, regardless of who we are in Christ. If we revert to the devices of the seed of Cain, even in an attempt to bring about the purposes of God, it will ultimately cause us much trouble.

Abraham was chosen by God to bring about His purposes. The promise he had received from God was true. The consequences of Abraham's self-seeking methods are still wreaking international havoc in the world today. "Ishmaels" brought forth by Christian ministries have been no less devastating to the Body of Christ. There is continual conflict between that which is born of the flesh and that which is born of the Spirit.

Because Ishmael was Abraham's son, The Lord blessed him and made him a great nation (Gen. 17:17-20), even though He knew that he was going to cause trouble for the promised seed. The Lord often blesses our spiritual Ishmaels as well, causing them to prosper. He will use them as much as He can and they may bless many people, but when "Isaac" appears, that which is born of the flesh must be driven out. Flesh cannot be an heir with that which is born of the Spirit.

Inevitably, one day the flesh will persecute that which is born of the Spirit. The flesh must be maintained by the flesh; striving, begging, pleading, and threatening. The more a minister has to strive to hold together a work, the more easily intimidated he will be by the appearance of anyone else in his domain. One never has to look far to see examples of this in the Body of Christ. The Lord foresaw this and exhorted that we would know the "true seed" by their love for one another.

Looking for a City

Because of God's call Abraham left the only land he had ever known. He did not know where he was going, **but he did know what he was looking for.** *"He was looking for a city which has foundations"* (Heb. 11:10).

It is the nature of God's call to separate us from all that we have known and built our lives upon. His call is the call to live by faith in Him alone. It is only by this faith that we can serve Him. His kingdom is not of this world. He is Spirit and if we are to serve Him we must serve Him in the Spirit. Faith is the door which He has provided for us to enter the spiritual realm. As our faith in Him increases, He becomes more real than the world and its forces of influence. Our service to Him will be pure and effective to our degree of single-mindedness. Our service will be corrupted to the degree that outside influences can affect us.

When Jesus was asked by His followers what they needed to do, His answer was pointed: *"This is the work of God, that you believe in Him whom He has sent"* (John 6:29). Our ultimate calling is to ultimately believe. But this faith is not blind and it is not naive; it is ultimate vision and understanding. Abraham did not know where he was going, but he knew exactly what he was looking for — and so must we. He was looking for a specific city; one which had *foundations*. We have been called to be a part of the same city. Our calling has substance; the faith we live by has substance, and the "city" we have been called to inhabit has more substance than all the futile works of man. If we settle for less, it is not true faith or the city God has built.

There is a fundamental principle of construction: the size and strength of any building will be determined by the size and strength of its foundation. If a man is going to build a small house or building, some shallow footings may be sufficient for a foundation. But if he plans to construct a large and strong building, he must do more than just dig footings. He will have to dig deep enough to find the bedrock, and even then he is not finished. He will have to drive pilings into the bedrock and fasten them securely to it. If he does not do this, the building can sink, tilt, or collapse under its own weight.

The same principles apply in spiritual matters. We must build down before we can build up. The amount of patience we have in building down will determine the greatness of that which can be built up. The ruins of ministries, churches, and individuals who failed to lay the proper foundations testify to the soberness of this issue.

Albert Einstein once made an observation that may be more important than his theory of relativity. He stated simply but profoundly that "Premature responsibility breeds superficiality". The Lord Jesus testified to this also. He said that the seed that sprouted too fast would have shallow roots. Contrary to this wisdom, we often esteem most highly those who develop the fastest. The result has been a serious weakening of many in the body of Christ.

It is crucial that we take the time and energy to lay the foundation properly, but it will be of little use if we do not lay the *right* foundation. Soon after my conversion I found myself in a congregation that emphasized the revelation of the Body of Christ. This is an exciting and important revelation, and I began to build my foundation on it. I added many other aspects of Christian truth to my life, but my emphasis was the Church. My "building" got bigger and bigger, and my ministry grew rapidly . . . then the whole thing began to tilt! I knew something was awry but could not figure out what it was. Everything seemed scriptural, and there was no major sin in my life; but I was striving more and more to keep everything from falling apart. Through wise counsel, the Lord revealed my foundational principles as true and right; but they were supposed to be a part of the *building*, not the foundation! I had been building upon the *things* of the Lord instead of upon the Lord. I began to drift into great extremes. The apostle declares:

> *No man can lay a foundation other than the One which is laid, which is Jesus Christ* (1 Cor. 3:11).

As wonderful as the revelations of God are, there is only ONE foundation — Jesus. If we build upon any other spiritual truth, it will never sustain the pressures of spiritual life. Sooner or later it will crumble and fall apart.

Many doctrines being taught today have drifted into extremes. Many of them began as timely revelations for the Body of Christ. Errors made in most cases were not inherent in the doctrine. The problem was in trying to build upon improper foundations. Some manage through sheer tenacity to get pretty far off before the whole structure collapses. Others recognize that something is wrong and start over with the right foundation.

Usually one will find the specific emphasis of a congregation to be its foundation. The apostles and preachers of the New Testament had only one message: Jesus. They preached all the doctrines preached today and maybe a few more — yet their whole message was based **in Him** *"in whom are hidden all of the treasures of wisdom and knowledge"* (Col. 2:3). In a broader sense, Jesus is not only the foundation: He is the whole building! All things are to be summed up in Him. Spiritual maturity is not just growing in the knowledge of certain spiritual truths; *"We are to grow up in all aspects into Him"* (Eph. 4:15). The apostles' labor was devoted to Christ being formed in His people. There is a big difference between this and trying to get people to conform to certain spiritual truths. A discerning historian noted the difference between Jesus and Caesar: Caesar sought to change men by changing laws and institutions; Jesus changed laws and institutions by changing men. Emphasizing externals may bring about a form of godliness but actually denies His power. Any emphasis that takes precedence over the Person of Jesus will lead to lifeless ritual. We must see everything through Him. When we seek to see Him through anything, then He will be distorted.

When the multitudes became hungry, Jesus gave them what they were seeking. He took *loaves*, broke them and gave them to the people. After they had eaten, only fragments remained (John 6:11-12). This is, in a sense, a picture of the Church. We have partaken of many different loaves (or emphases) and all that has been left are fragments. Just as Jesus sought to turn the attention of the multitude to the one Loaf, Himself, so He is seeking to turn our attention from varied doctrines to Him. *"In Him do all things hold together"* (Col. 1:17). In Him there are no fragments; in Him all doctrines are found in perfect harmony. Taught as isolated extremes, even the greatest spiritual truths will leave the church in fragments. Seen through Him, all doctrines take their appropriate perspective and balance, and can be taught without creating division. *"God, after He spoke long ago to the fathers in the prophets in many portions and in many ways* (the loaves), *in these last days has spoken to us in His Son* (the one Loaf)" (Heb. 1:1-2).

We see this truth illustrated again in Martha after the death of her brother Lazarus. Martha understood accurately the doctrine of resurrection. She knew that her brother would rise again on the last day; but her hope was in the **doctrine** of the resurrection, not in Jesus. He redirected her hope: *"I am the Resurrection"*, He explained (John 11:25). But He is not **just** the resurrection: He is the Truth; He is all truth. He is the revelation from God and of God. He is *I AM*.

If doctrine becomes our emphasis, we are being led astray. We are not changed by doctrine; we are changed by seeing Jesus (2 Cor. 3:18). Anointed teachings are essential for the nourishment of the Christ that is being formed within us, but whenever a truth becomes our focus, it will lead us astray. For this reason Satan often comes as an angel of light, or "messenger of truth". Truth can deceive us.

Only in *the* Truth, Jesus, is there life. He did not come just to teach us truth; He came to *be* Truth.

In Exodus 33:8-11, we see Moses in the tent of meeting speaking to the Lord. A pillar of cloud would descend and the Lord would speak to Moses face to face just as a man speaks to his friend. It was such an awesome sight that all the people would arise and stand at the doorways of their tents to worship when this meeting took place. When Moses returned to the camp, Joshua (who was at that time Moses' personal servant) would remain in the tent of meeting. Joshua was staying to develop his *own* relationship to the Lord. Being the most intimate associate of a man of God was not enough for Joshua — **he had to know the Lord for himself**. It may have been for this reason that Joshua was chosen to lead Israel into the promised land.

When we have a great man or woman of God to relate to, we become spiritually lulled. Because of this, many of the great moves of God begin and end with the leaders. How numerous are the institutions, schools, churches, and missions that have ceased with the death of their founders? After Joshua died, Israel lapsed into spiritual decadence. Few revivals last more than a generation after the initial move of the Spirit. The primary reason for this is that men (or doctrine) became the foundation upon which the movement was based. Only when Jesus is the foundation will a move of the Spirit last. The Spirit came to testify of Jesus, not His ministers or doctrines — but Jesus! When we turn to anything else we will quickly head down side alleys that will never lead us to life.

Before Jesus sent anyone out to minister, He first called them to Himself. He did not send them to the finest Bible college or make them take a correspondence course. He said, *"Follow Me"*. The light that was in Him was to become the light that was in them. This is still His call to those who would be His disciples — *"Follow Me"*. We must respond to Him as the Shulamite maid in the Song of Solomon (who is a type of the bride of Christ).

Tell me, O You whom my soul loves, Where do you pasture your flock . . . for why should I be like one of those who veils herself beside the flocks of your companions (Song of Sol. 1:7)

Jesus *alone* is the mediator between God and man (1 Tim. 2:5). *"Christ is the Head of every man"* (1 Cor. 11:3). The leaders and ministers that He gives to His church are never meant to take His place; they are given to lead us to Him. The Lord has ordained men as elders and pastors, but they are exhorted to *"shepherd the flock of God"* (1 Pet. 5:2), not set up their own flocks. Throughout the history of the church, there have been those who have become veils between the Lord and His people by seeking to establish believers as their own flocks. Foreseeing this, the Lord promised when He brought His people together they would be *"One flock with one Shepherd"* (John 10:16). The ministry of those who are true under-shepherds is not to establish their own authority over the Lord's people, but His. Those who have used this ministry to establish their domains will be greatly ashamed as The Chief Shepherd warned:

> *But do not be called Rabbi; for One is your Teacher, and you are all brothers.*

> *And do not call anyone on earth your father; for One is your Father, He who is in Heaven.*

> *And do not be called leaders; for One is your Leader, that is Christ.*

> *But the greatest among you shall be your servant.*

> *And whoever exalts himself (to presume beyond this exhortation) shall be humbled; and whoever humbles himself shall be exalted* (Matt. 23:8-12).

John the Baptist is a wonderful type of spiritual ministry. The focus of his entire mission was to reveal Jesus. It was his delight to decrease as Jesus increased. Because of that humility he was greatly exalted by the Lord Himself as He declared John to be the greatest man ever born of woman (Matt. 11:11). When we have seen and borne witness of the Son of God as John did, it is a delight to decrease in our ministry as He increases. All spiritual labor is for the purpose of Christ being formed in His people. When we see this taking place, there is no greater joy. It is the seal and testimony that we have been abiding in the Vine so as to bear fruit. The true friends of the Bridegroom rejoice to see His day, even if it means the end of their own ministry.

When John the Baptist saw Jesus passing, he exhorted his disciples to *"Behold the Lamb of God!"* (John 1:36). Hearing this, John and Andrew left the Baptist and began to follow Jesus. When He perceived them following, He turned and asked them what may be the most important question that we ever consider. *"What do you seek?"* (verse 38). This is one question that sooner or later we will all be required to answer. Why are *we* following Him? John and Andrew answered with another question, but it was possibly the most appropriate reply: *"Lord, where do you dwell?"* Hearing this Jesus beckoned them to do what has been the heart's desire of every true seeker of God since Enoch: *"Come and you will see"* (verse 39). We do not have to settle for reading about it, or hearing the testimonies of those who have gone; Jesus came to bid each of us to follow Him and see for ourselves where He dwells. This dwelling is not a physical place; He was speaking of the Kingdom of God.

The next day Andrew became the first evangelist in history: he found his brother Simon Peter and declared Jesus to be the Messiah (verses 41 and 42). He did not try to convince Simon with a lengthy discourse from the scriptures; he did not even share the four spiritual laws with him — he simply *"brought him to Jesus"* (John 1:42).

If we are led to Jesus, and not just to the Church or doctrine, we have come to the only true foundation. Then, like Peter, our faith will grow. Peter was an uneducated, simple fisherman, yet he stood before the most powerful and educated men of his nation and astonished them with his authority and dignity. Peter's faith was not built upon participation in an institution or teachings; **he knew Jesus.** There is no formula given for salvation — it is a Person. Truth is not just a systematic theology — it is Jesus. He came to be our life. He is the deepest desire of the human heart. Only in Him do we really begin to live.

5

Jacob & Esau, Reuben & Joseph

I have loved Jacob, but I have hated (Lit. "opposed") *Esau*
(Mal. 1:2-3)

This scripture has been difficult for many believers. Why would
the Lord favor a lying, cheating, deceiving schemer like Jacob over
a nice guy like Esau, who loved and obeyed his parents and exuded
such godliness? This seems totally incongruous. But God does not
look at the outward character; He looks on the heart. Esau may
have had a strong external character, but he was weak in spirit. He
proved more concerned about his appetite than his eternal inheritance in Christ. He traded his birthright as the firstborn of Isaac
for a single bowl of stew! This was an affront to God. The
flippancy of Esau's attitude may shock us, but the same nature
dwells within us.

The Lord Jesus purchased with His precious blood the opportunity to dwell before the very throne of God. How easily we trade
this privilege! We constantly spend time before a worthless
television program or a multitude of other distractions that are
worth even less than the stew! This is within us. We will thought-
lessly trade away our eternal birthright in Christ for temporary,
carnal gratification.

In contrast to Esau, Jacob so highly valued the birthright that
he would risk his life to attain it. In many ways, he may have been
more carnal than Esau, but his heart burned for the inheritance in
Christ. He was determined to obtain God's blessing, even if he had
to wrestle with God to get it; which eventually he did (Gen.
32:24-32).

To wrestle with God in rebellion is folly. To wrestle with Him for our inheritance is a determination He longs to see in His people. Jacob determined he was going to lay hold of the Lord and not let Him go until he had received the blessing. How contrary this is to the way we often seek the Lord! We may offer a hasty or impulsive prayer, or settle down to what we call "serious prayer" (should there be any prayer that isn't serious?); but if we do not soon receive, we often assume it was not God's will and give up. The Lord exhorted through Jeremiah: *"you will seek Me and find Me, when you search for Me with all your heart"* (Jer. 29:13). The Lord wants us to seek Him and **find** Him! He would be doing us a great disservice if His blessing was easily attainable. This would only feed our slothfulness in spiritual matters. He often makes Himself difficult to find so that we will have to search for Him harder. He is like the parent who teaches his child to walk by backing away so the child will have to take more steps to reach him. He wants to bring us to the place where we are seeking Him all the time with all our heart. But instead of taking more steps to reach Him, we often give up and "sit down", thus not reaching Him at all.

The Lord never wants us to stop seeking Him until we have found Him. He wants to answer all our prayers. To some of them the answer may be "no" but we should never stop seeking Him until we have heard from Him. Silence is not an answer to prayer. If He were to answer some of our half-hearted prayers, it would be detrimental to our spiritual growth. We must not give up until we have found Him.

Jacob would not give up in seeking the blessing and he received it. Not only did he receive the blessing he sought, but his nature was changed. To signify this, the Lord changed his name from Jacob, which means "usurper" to Israel, which means "a prince with God"; because he had *"striven with God and with men and [had] prevailed"* (Gen. 32:28). If we persistently seek the Lord, we too will find Him, and when we do, our nature will also be changed from that of Cain to the nature of His Son. Then we too will be "a Prince with God".

Reuben, Jacob's firstborn, had the same nature as his uncle Esau. He allowed his flesh to rob him of his inheritance. His carnal appetite drove him to defile his father's bed. When Jacob blessed his sons before passing away, he only had a rebuke for Reuben:

> *Reuben, you are my first-born; my might and the beginning of my strength. Preeminent in dignity and preeminent in power. **Uncontrolled as water, you shall not have preeminence*** (Gen. 49:3-4).

Like Esau, Reuben may have been preeminent in dignity and power, but he was ruled by his flesh and it cost him dearly. The lack of self-control began in the garden and is still today robbing many of their eternal inheritance in Christ. We are our own greatest enemy.

Dust in scripture is typical of the carnal nature of man, or the "flesh" (Adam was made from the dust). The curse upon the serpent was that he would eat the dust (Gen. 3:14); or Satan was to feed on the carnal nature of man. Satan's dominion over man is perpetuated by man's carnal nature. Through the ages one of Satan's most successful tactics for robbing God's people of their inheritance has been to offer them the immediate gratification of their flesh. This tactic has been so successful that he even tried it on Jesus. Knowing that Jesus was to be the heir of the world, but also knowing the testing and consecration required before receiving God's fulfillment of His promises, he proposed an easier way. Satan proposed that if Jesus would bow down and worship him, he would give Him the world immediately: no cross, no suffering, and no waiting. By this same seductive deception, Satan has induced many saints to take the "easy" way . . . to their ultimate, eternal consternation. The invitation to worship Satan is seldom blatant enough to be perceived as such; it is usually simply an invitation to take the wider, more traveled path.

The way of God is a very narrow, difficult path, and there are no shortcuts. *"Through many tribulations we must enter the kingdom of God"* (Acts 14:22). Many doctrines have suggested to the Body of Christ an easier way, but they do not lead to the Kingdom. To walk with God is to walk against the tide of the whole human race, and when a man walks against the tide, he is bound to make waves. As we have clearly been told: *"All who desire to live godly in Christ Jesus will be persecuted"* (2 Tim. 3:12). Satan is forever inducing us to relax and flow with the tide to avoid persecution and misunderstanding. Only those who love their calling more than they love comfort and acceptance can stand.

The Church has been decimated because of lack of discipline and self-control; but a problem possibly more destructive has been our uncanny knack of accepting weak spiritual leaders. Usually this is because they appear to be "preeminent in dignity and strength". Paul observed this tendency in the Corinthian church: *"You bear with anyone if he enslaves you, if he takes advantage of you, if he hits you in the face"* (2 Cor. 11:20). Carnal men respond to carnal strength. We are still quick to follow anyone who appears to be head and shoulders above others.

To judge by externals is a common error, and is a great temptation even for those who are intimate with the Lord. The great prophet Samuel had a difficult time learning this lesson. One would think after the fiasco with Saul he would not be so quick to judge another king by physical appearance. But after the Lord sent him to the house of Jesse to anoint a successor, he succumbed to the same temptation:

> *Then it came about when he entered, that he looked at Eliab and thought, "Surely this is the Lord's anointed".*

> *But the Lord said to Samuel, "Do not look at his appearance or at the height of his stature, because I have rejected him; for the Lord sees not as man sees, for man looks at the outward appearance, but God looks at the heart"* (1 Sam. 16:6-7).

Many who are "Preeminent in dignity and preeminent in strength" are "uncontrolled as water" and weak in spiritual strength. The Lord's strength is made perfect in weakness (2 Cor. 12:9). *"God has chosen the weak things of the world to shame the things that are strong"* (1 Cor. 1:27). Neither natural strengths nor intellectual and social prowess are requirements for spiritual leadership. Such qualities may even be hindrances. This is not to advocate that we should only look for the physically weak or intellectually slow to be our spiritual leaders; but we should not judge by externals, period! It is critical that we are sensitive to the Spirit as to whom He has chosen. Natural abilities cannot bring forth the fruit of the Spirit.

He often chooses the weak or slow so His perfect wisdom and power may be evident.

> *We are the true circumcision who worship in the Spirit of God and glory in Christ Jesus and put no confidence in the Flesh* (Phil. 3:3).

The Lord declared through the prophet Isaiah the demeanor of the ones whom He would choose:

> *Thus says the Lord, "Heaven is My throne and the earth is MY footstool. Where then is the house you could build for Me? And where is the place that I may rest?*

> *"For My hand made all these things, thus all these things came into being," declares the Lord. "but to this one will I look* (to be His habitation), *to him who is humble and contrite of spirit, and who trembles at My word"* (Is. 66:1-2).

True humility is a prerequisite to being a vessel of the Lord. It was the pride of man that allowed him to presume he could be like God. It is this same pride that continues to separate us from Him. When we see Him as He is, this presumption is stopped cold. The clamoring of the world's great and mighty seems pitiful and absurd when we see the Lord in His glory. The world's most righteous men are utterly humiliated when they behold the Lord. The "greatest man born of woman" did not consider himself worthy to even untie His shoes. Where is the house that we can build for Him? The greatest human talent cannot accomplish His work. Only the Spirit can beget that which is Spirit. He does not call us for our strengths — He calls us for our weaknesses. Just as our Lord Jesus emptied Himself to become a servant, He looks for those who will have no confidence in the flesh and become a vessel for His Spirit.

Because of the pride of man, the Lord puts His treasures in that which is repulsive. Even Jesus, the Lord and creator of the universe, was birthed in a stable and reared in the most despised town in the most despised nation on earth. Prophetically we were told that *"He has no stately form or majesty that we should look upon*

Him, nor appearance that we should be attracted to Him" (Is. 53:2).
To receive Him thusly, we would have to renounce our pride. He
is seeking those who are not attracted by externals, but the Spirit.
Men in their pride rejected the One who is the very cornerstone of
creation. To the degree that we follow our pride (or trust in carnal
abilities of man) we will reject Him. If we are to be the sons of
God we must be led by the Spirit of God. *"From now on we
recognize no man according to the flesh"* (2 Cor. 5:16).

Reuben, Jacob's firstborn, abounded in strength and dignity but
lacked inner fortitude. Joseph was next to the youngest and
despised by his brothers, yet God chose him to inherit the birthright
of the firstborn:

> *Now the sons of Reuben, the firstborn of Israel (For he was the
> firstborn, but because he defiled his father's bed, his birthright
> was given to the sons of Joseph, the son of Israel; so that he
> was not enrolled in the genealogy according to birthright.*
>
> *Though Judah prevailed over his brothers, and through him was
> the leader, yet the birthright belonged to Joseph)* (1 Chron.
> 5:1-2).

Reuben committed the detestable act of lying with his father's
wife, which cost him his birthright. In contrast Joseph, under the
most tempting circumstances, remained faithful. He refused his
master's wife's advances even though this meant imprisonment.
This — after Joseph had already suffered incredible personal
injustices. He faced situations which would have weakened any
person's resolve in a land that was void of the most basic moral
standards. But Joseph had a law in his heart that was stronger than
external circumstances and temptations. A type of the Messiah that
was to come, Joseph was rejected by his brothers but became the
cornerstone of their salvation.

Body, Soul and Spirit

Man is basically made up of three parts: body, soul and spirit.
The body is composed of the elements of the earth. As the popular

statement contends: "We are what we eat." To maintain a healthy body we need a proper diet and proper exercise. However, our natural tendency is toward junk food, which does not satisfy the basic nutritional needs of our bodies; and we tend to be lazy and not exercise. Discipline is required to maintain a healthy diet and proper exercise.

The soul of man is composed of our intellect, emotions and will. The soul, like the body, is going to become what we feed it. It too has a tendency to desire "junk food" and get out of shape. Every seed that is sown in our minds will be reaped (Gal. 6:7). What we allow ourselves to read, think, hear or see is critical to soul health. We must be disciplined in attaining the proper intellectual exercise.

Contrarily, the spirit of regenerated man has a tendency toward God. But it too must have proper diet and exercise. Jesus said, *"The words that I have spoken to you are spirit and life"* (John 6:63).

The very weak are ruled by their bodies. They are controlled by impulses, habits and fleshly desires. We could include Esau and Reuben in this category. Others are ruled by the soul — emotions, feelings and opinions. But the Lord has called us to walk by the *Spirit*. *"For all who are being led by the Spirit of God these are sons of God"* (Rom. 8:14). The Lord desires for us to have a healthy body, soul and spirit subjected to His Spirit.

When we first commit ourselves to the Lord we inevitably emphasize correction in areas of our lives that belong to the body and soul. In most cases there are problems in these areas that do need immediate attention. However, the body and soul are not meant to be the focus of our attention. Before becoming Christians, most of us are totally unaware of the spiritual aspect of our constitution. Sadly, many Christians remain unaware of their spiritual nature throughout their lives. The overwhelming emphasis concerning spiritual growth actually has been the soul realm — knowledge, wisdom, understanding and discipline of the will. These are important and I would not want to detract from them, but there is much more to our life in Christ!

> *But an hour is coming, and now is, when the true worshipers shall worship the Father in spirit and truth; for such people the Father seeks to be His worshipers.*

*God is Spirit; and those who worship Him **must** worship in spirit and truth* (John 4:23-24).

The Lord said that His words are **spirit** and life. He said His sheep know His voice. This is possibly the most important aspect of our lives — knowing His voice. Those led by the Spirit of God are the sons of God. We are not to be led by impulses, feelings or reasoning. This has caused others to shy away from attempting to follow the Spirit at all, citing excesses and mistakes. There is a straight and narrow path that leads to true life. One can live by all the principles and rules in the Bible, human reasoning and whatever may sustain emotional equilibrium but be far from the will of God. It is essential that we know His voice and are led by His Spirit if we are to be His.

6

Pharaoh and Moses

Pharaoh is a type of Satan, the present ruler of the world system. He is another personification of the seed of the serpent. In him we see many of the same devices that Satan uses to keep God's people in bondage. We also see in Pharaoh the oppressive authority rooted in the selfish ambitions of the rebellious nature.

Moses, on the other hand, is a type of Christ who has come to set God's people free. As he prophetically explained to Israel: *"The Lord your God will raise up for you a prophet like me, from your countrymen, you shall listen to Him"* (Deut. 18:15). He was explaining that his life was a foreshadowing of the prophet, Jesus, who was to come. We can easily see the parallels in their lives. When Moses was born Pharaoh issued a decree to destroy all the male children born to Israel (Ex. 1:22). Herod sought to destroy Jesus by having all the male children in Bethlehem killed. The first time Moses revealed himself to his people, they rejected him as their savior just as Jesus was rejected the first time He came to Israel. The second time Moses came was with great power. There are many other examples in the life and ministry of Moses that were prophetic parallels of Jesus. In Moses we also have a wonderful example of the self-sacrificing nature of true spiritual authority as opposed to the self-seeking nature of human authority.

Under Pharaoh's dominion, Israel was in slavery and subjected to toil. The Lord sent Moses to set Israel free and bring them into a land flowing with milk and honey that they might find rest. We distinguish here between the kingdom of this world and the kingdom of God. One kingdom is seeking to increase the bondage of its subjects while the other seeks to set men free. In this world, little is accomplished without toil. (This is not speaking of labor; man labored in the garden {cultivated it} before the fall and the curse of toil was the result of transgression {Gen. 2:15}.) Toil is work that is accomplished only with **great and painful** effort. We labor in the kingdom of God, but the Lord's yoke is easy and His burden is light. In His kingdom, far more is accomplished with less effort. All toil brings weariness, but the labor in Christ, regardless of whether it is a secular or spiritual endeavor, brings rest and refreshment:

> *Take My yoke upon you, and learn from Me, for I am gentle and humble in heart; and you shall find rest for your souls* (Matt. 11:29).

The attempts of Satan to enslave us are often very subtle; at times they even have the appearance of liberty. But the "freedom" of this world always leads to bondage. *"They promise freedom while they themselves are slaves to corruption: for by what a man is overcome, by this he is enslaved"* (2 Pet. 2:19). The present trend towards sexual freedom is a good example of this. The more "free" one becomes in his pursuit of satisfaction, the less satisfaction he experiences. Soon this "freedom" becomes a compulsion to seek satisfaction in new and different experiences. These only increase the appetite while providing less and less fulfillment, until only perversions seem interesting. Then the degree of perversion must be increased until one is finally consumed and ultimately destroyed seeking satisfaction.

In Christ the opposite is true. What externally appears to be bondage is what actually sets us free. He created the sexual appetite of man to be fulfilled. The first thing that God said referred to man's need for companionship, so He created woman to correspond (Lit. "fit together") with man (Gen. 2:18). The fitting together is not just physical, but encompasses soul and spirit as well. Sexual intercourse is only one level of interrelation the Lord designated between man and woman. All of them lead to UNION. The Lord instituted marriage and prohibited sexual intercourse outside marriage so we would experience the fulfillment we are truly seeking — union in soul, spirit and body.

Whenever we enter into sexual intercourse with selfish motives, we are even more alone than we were before. The loneliness increases our appetite for union, which is usually translated into a need for more sexual intercourse. Lust is a self-perpetuating cycle that becomes more intense as it continues. Sexual intercourse that is born out of love and *commitment* to the union helps profoundly to enhance the relationship. Of course, marriage does not guarantee the proper use of this gift, but sex is *never* utilized properly outside of marriage. Through the union experienced in marriage, we begin to understand the greater union of Christ and His church . . . the yearning of our spirits to be joined with Him. In our union with Him is satisfaction and fulfillment the world cannot comprehend. It is the fulfillment of the purpose for which we were created.

Everything pertaining to life and godliness is provided for us in Christ (2 Pet. 1:3). We can only be fulfilled in Him. Every perversion of human nature is caused by man's attempt to find fulfillment and security, which only leads to dissatisfaction and insecurity. Loneliness is a root of much evil. There is within all the *need* to *fit*, to be united with creation. The kingdom of God is the ultimate symphony: the harmony of the Creator with His creation. The essential need to be harmonious is basic to all creation, but man has distorted this through determining to seek fulfillment on his own. The more removed one becomes from overall harmony, the more assertive his importance and position. As one attains willful authority in this manner, he becomes paranoid and insecure. His attempts only lead to greater need and dissatisfaction. Until God's kingdom comes, men will incessantly form clubs, societies and boards in order to "feel a part". There will be a striving for rank and recognition. To some degree this appeases their basic need. Those who have truly become united with Christ and His purposes have no need for such pettiness. To one who has found fulfillment in Him there is equal willingness to become least or greatest. Rank is not important . . . fruit is. United purpose overshadows position.

The Fear of Rejection

When man has not been redeemed and reunited with Christ, he carries the rejection of Cain. Man *is not* acceptable to God except in Jesus. Just as Cain's sacrifice of his own works was rejected, those propagated through Cain know deep inside they are not acceptable. Fear of rejection is probably the most dominant force within those who have not been "crucified with Christ". It is not good for man to be alone; yet this fear of rejection causes people to shy away from the very thing they need for fulfillment. Fear causes man to put up facades of independence and self-sufficiency to protect him from possible rejection. Often these facades cause rejection that in turn causes one to be even more aloof. It is a vicious cycle.

Cain was rejected because he sought God on his own terms — the presumption that caused the perversion of man's spirit in the first place. After the fall, this attitude was to prevail, deeply rooted in disharmony. The insecure are threatened by that which they cannot control. As man is further removed from what he needs most (union), insecurity increases. Relationships are reduced to devices used to manipulate and control. They are not unions but wars, often held together by the greater fear of being left completely alone. When we enter a union with terms that demand our control, those terms prohibit true union. True union cannot take place while self-seeking and self preservation are involved. These are barriers that will separate us from one another and the Lord — true union requires the total giving of oneself to the other. Only when we lay down all barriers and facades in order to give are we open to really receive. We must first lose our life if we are to find it.

In Christ the rejection of Cain is taken away. In Him we come to know God's acceptance, which is greater than any other. In His love we are secure. We are able to trust Him because His cross proved He has our best interest in mind. As we become secure in His Lordship and control, the compulsion to control other people and circumstances is reduced until we are ultimately able to enter the "sabbath rest" of God. Only then are we truly fit to serve in positions of authority.

When one is controlled by fear every perception is distorted. Until there is restoration of union with God, man is utterly alone. He may have relationships with others but true union is not possible until the perfect love of God has cast out all his fears. To the fearful the world is a threat and life is a battle to gain control. When the fearful gain control of a situation it is oppression. Fear causes overreactions to real or perceived threats to one's position.

There is an old adage that states: "Power corrupts; absolute power corrupts absolutely". This is true for those who seek authority but have not come under the authority of Christ. The lust for power is fueled by the insecurity of man; his drive for control is often a defense mechanism to protect him from rejection. But power over others will never allay fears; it will only increase them. The more we strive to maintain dominion over our little kingdoms, the greater the burdens become. It's only when we have "lost our lives" (our claims to dominion) and surrendered dominion to Christ that we find life and freedom. All who achieve power without knowing the love of God are open to paranoia. The lightest deviation from doctrine or the smallest expression of free-thinking becomes absurdly sinister. Those who have truly surrendered to Christ will not be intimidated by challenges or dismayed by rejection. If we have remorse, it will not be because we are threatened or misunderstood but because many are deceived and do not know Him. Those who exercise authority with selfish motives are corrupt, regardless of pretentious piety. Those truly surrendered to Christ will handle authority with the greatest care, knowing they are His servants.

The typical reaction of Cain's seed is seen in Pharaoh. When Moses sought freedom for Israel, Pharaoh made the burdens on his slaves heavier (Ex. 5:9). With every attempt at freedom by underlings, the seed of Cain will become more oppressive and his fears more irrational. There is inherent corruption in authority apart from God.

The Lord created man to rule over the fish of the sea, the birds of the air, and every living thing that creeps on the earth (Gen. 1:28); but it was not originally His purpose for men to rule over other men. He alone was to be man's authority. When man resisted His rule and chose to go his own way, the Lord established men over other men to keep the world from being reduced to utter chaos. For this reason the apostles exhorted the Church to be subject to all earthly authority:

Let every person be in subjection to the governing authorities.
For there is no authority except from God, and those which
exist are established by God. Therefore he who resists authority
has opposed the ordinance of God; and they who have opposed
will receive condemnation upon themselves. For rulers are not
a cause of fear for good behavior, but for evil. Do you want to
have no fear of authority? Do what is good and you will have
praise from the same; for it is a minister of God to you for
good. But if you do what is evil, be afraid; for it does not bear
the sword for nothing; for it is a minister of God, an avenger
who brings wrath upon the one who practices evil (Rom.
13:1-4).

Submit yourself for the Lord's sake to every human institution,
whether to a king as the one in authority, or to governors as
sent by him for the punishment of evil doers and the praise of
those who do right (1 Pet. 2:13-14).

Even though there have been many dictators, kings and
presidents in which the spirit of evil has been apparent, no one is
established authoritatively unless God allows it. We may not
understand the Lord's purpose in many things, but every authority
that He permits to come to power is to bring about His purposes.
He understands the inherent corruption in power as it is exercised
by the unredeemed; therefore He exhorts His people to pray for all
who are in authority. If we, without God's grace, were subject to
the same pressures and temptations as those in authority, we would
stumble terribly. They should receive our support even when others
desert them. This is not to say that if the Nazis come to power, we
attend their rallies and give them lists of all the Jews we know . . .
obviously there are exceptions. When the Sanhedrin demanded that
the apostles stop preaching in the name of Jesus, their reply was
"We must obey God rather than men" (Acts 5:29). God may overrule
all authority of men. When His authority is in conflict with men's,
we must obey Him first. This is, however, the only time we should
disobey established authorities.

Even though King Saul had become possessed with an evil spirit
and God had declared that He was going to remove him, David's
heart smote him because he cut off the edge of Saul's robe. David's

fear of touching anyone ordained by the Lord was greater than personal resentment or ambition. David had already been anointed king in Saul's place, yet he refused to take this authority by his own hand. This faith in the Lord's righteous judgement and perfect ways is a primary reason the Lord promised David his kingdom would endure forever. Had he taken the authority by his hand, he would have been subject to equal retribution. To the degree we strive in our own strength to attain even that which God has appointed for us, to that degree our authority will be weakened. Though the authority of the world is subject to the corruption of fallen man, we must submit ourselves to it "for conscience sake" (the same conscience that smote David for touching Saul's robe). We may have to disobey civil authorities under certain circumstances, but we are not to oppose it, because *"God is the judge; He puts down one and exalts another"* (Ps. 75:7).

Though God did not originally ordain men to rule over men, until all has been restored it is necessary. Primary to the whole Church age was testing and refining those faithful followers who would rule with Him over men in the age to come. This reign is to last a thousand years (Rev. 20:4), at which time all things will again have been made subject to Him (1 Cor. 15:28). After the thousand-year day of the Lord is completed, *"they shall not teach again, each man his neighbor and each man his brother, saying 'know the Lord', for they shall all know Me, from the least of them to the greatest of them, declares the Lord"* (Jer. 31:34). This was the original plan — that we would all know the Lord intimately and be responsible to Him; and this is the condition to which man will return. All authority the Lord establishes for and through His people is toward this end. I am not speaking of authority that is established to keep order until the kingdom of God comes . . . they are fundamentally different and are established to bring about different ends, as the Lord Jesus testified:

> *You know that the rulers of the Gentiles lord it over them, and their great men exercise authority over them. It is not so among you, but whoever wishes to become great among you shall be your servant, and whoever wishes to be first among you shall be your slaves; just as the Son of Man did not come to be*

served, but to serve, and to give His life a ransom for many (Matt. 20:25-28).

The Lord was not here condemning Gentile authority; indeed, He established it! But He made it clear that kingdom authority was of a different nature.

There are two kinds of leaders: those who use people for their own interests and those who sacrifice themselves for the interests of the people. The former denotes the nature of worldly authority; the latter godly authority. Pharaoh allowed his country to be destroyed while striving to preserve his power over the Jews. In Moses we have a striking contrast to Pharaoh's self-centeredness and a wonderful example of kingdom authority: as Israel continually resisted and rejected him, Moses so loved and identified with these people that he offered his own life to appease God's wrath on them. Such is the nature of all who are truly exercising authority in the Spirit of Jesus.

> *Have this attitude in yourselves which was also in Christ Jesus, who, although He existed in the form of God, did not regard equality with God a thing to be grasped, but **emptied Himself**, taking the form of a bond servant, and being made in the likeness of men. And being found in appearance as a man, He humbled Himself by becoming obedient to the point of death, even death on a cross* (the most humiliating death possible). *Therefore God highly exalted Him, and bestowed on Him the name which is above every name; that at the name of Jesus every knee should bow* (Phil. 2:3-10).

For the seed of Cain, authority is an opportunity for self-promotion and self-exaltation. In Christ the call to authority is the call to self-sacrifice; it is the call to become a slave and to give up one's interests. To rule in Christ is not self-gratifying; it is self-emptying. In Christ we do not serve in order to make a reputation but to become of "no reputation" (see Phil. 2:7, KJV). While Pharaoh was one of the most arrogant of all men, attempting even to fight against God, it was said that Moses was *"the most humble man on the face of the earth"* (Num. 12:3).

Selfish ambition is one of the most destructive characteristics found in ministry and has led to incredible perversion. When men are established in positions of authority prematurely, it is a tragedy for both leader and led. To be placed in spiritual authority before one has been freed from carnality will only feed that nature and may well prevent true spiritual authority. "Premature responsibility breeds superficiality."

Authority has been an issue in the body of Christ for the last decade. Though this issue has caused strife and confusion, it has challenged many to understand the true nature of spiritual authority. A lesson learned by many was not to follow the first doctrine that appears outstanding. Many doctrines are born out of sincerity, but a human perspective led Israel to cry for a king and Saul was the result. The Lord was going to give Israel a king at the proper time (the Lord had raised up the prophet Samuel specifically to prepare Israel for the coming king), but the people could not wait for God's chosen time. Sadly, it seems that this is repeated every time the Lord is about to move in a special way. Men begin to perceive the need because God is preparing them, but their impatience causes them to press the Lord before the perfect time. For this reason it seems there has always been a doctrinal Ishmael before Isaac or a Saul before David. The Lord time after time chose the younger son to be the heir of His promises over the older as a testimony that the earthly would always be born before the spiritual.

We can only have spiritual authority to the degree that the King lives within us. Paul said that he waited until it pleased the Father to reveal His Son *in* him, not just *to* him, before he began his ministry (Gal. 1:15-17). In this same discourse he declared that he did not immediately consult with flesh and blood about the matter. He received his message from the Lord and then after fourteen years he went to Jerusalem for confirmation concerning his message (see Gal. 1:15-17). In an abundance of counselors there is victory (Prov. 11:14). Submission to the body of Christ and the presbytery is important, but over-emphasizing this can greatly compromise ministry. The essential factor in fruitfulness of ministry is union with the Lord, not union with the Body. There are many bodies of Christians that claim to be Christ's but are not joined to Him. Paul warned us about ministries *"not holding fast to the Head"* (Col.

2:19). He gave no warnings about those who were not submitted to the Body.

Many "lone rangers" have made glaring failures of their ministries and lives. Some have contended this resulted from not being submitted to the authority of the Church. To a degree this may be true, but there have been many who were in submission to church authorities and have fallen just as severely. In contrast, history is filled with testimonies of individuals, completely isolated from fellow believers, that have endured incredible tests and remained faithful. Some doctrines of submission to spiritual authority are actually counterproductive in preparing individuals to be faithful and obedient to the Lord. This is not to promote individualism and spiritual independence, but when the emphasis of submission to the Body exceeds submission to the Lord, grave consequences have resulted. Some of the most anointed ministries the Lord has given His Church in our time have been rejected by large portions of the body of Christ because they did not emphasize their Body-union as Christ-union. Nowhere in scripture is there an exhortation to beware of those who are not submitted to other men.

Spirituality cannot be transferred by osmosis. An obvious example of this is the case of Paul and Gamaliel. In Acts 22 Paul declared himself to to have been a disciple of Gamaliel, therefore one would expect him to be like his teacher. However, while Paul was sitting under Gamaliel, we see a great contrast. Gamaliel's counsel to the Sanhedrin in Acts 5 contains amazing depth of patience and wisdom. When the rest of the council intended to slay the apostles for teaching in the name of Jesus, Gamaliel wisely suggested that they leave them alone *"for if this plan or action should be of men, it will be overthrown; but if it is of God, you will not be able to overthrow them; or else you may even be found fighting against God"* (verses 38-39). But what was Paul's reaction? *"I persecuted this Way to the death"* (Acts 22:4). Men cannot change other men. We may be able to affect outward behavior to some degree, but only the Holy Spirit can change a person's heart. There is a place for discipleship, but molding another's life is a grave and delicate matter. There is no recipe for imparting one's life and wisdom to another; it must be a Spirit-ordained and guided relationship.

It has become very easy for one to be rightly related to the Body (according to the popular interpretation) and have almost no relationship with the Lord. To be rightly related to the Lord is the most important element in every life and ministry. The Church cannot save, it cannot heal, it cannot baptize with the Holy Spirit, it cannot lead us into all truth. Only the Lord can do these things. When our emphasis becomes the Church more than the Lord, we have been reduced to worshipping the creation instead of the blessed Creator, and our faith has been reduced to a form of godliness which denies the very power of the gospel. We are not changed by beholding the Church; we are changed as we behold the Lord (2 Cor. 3:18). It is only after we have been united with the Lord that there can be a *real* union with His body. In beholding the Head, the Body is joined (Col. 2:19).

Knowing God's Ways

King David made a profound observation when he declared that the Lord *"made known His ways to Moses, His acts to the sons of Israel"* (Ps. 103:7). It was not enough for Moses to see the acts of the Lord; he longed to know His ways. This desire led him to become one of the most discerning spiritual leaders of all time. Moses reveals why knowing the Lord's ways are so important:

> *Then Moses said to the Lord, "See, Thou dost say to me, 'Bring up this people!' But Thou Thyself has not let me know whom Thou wilt send with me. Moreover, Thou hast said, 'I have known you by name, and you have also found favor in My sight.' Now therefore, I pray Thee, if I have found favor in Thy sight, let me know Thy ways, that I may know Thee, so that I might find favor in Thy sight* (Ex. 33:12-13).

Moses knew that he could properly lead God's people if he knew His ways; and only in knowing the Lord's ways could He know Him. He was called to lead God's people. They could not be led in the same way that other people might be led. The world's ways are not God's ways, and neither can they accomplish the Lord's purposes. This is a most crucial matter for the leadership of the body of Christ to understand. So often we have appointed leaders in the Church because of what they have attained in the world. Being a leader in the world may actually hinder spiritual leadership. Natural abilities and talents will mislead us if we depend on them in spiritual matters. That which is flesh is flesh; only that which is born of the Spirit can bring forth that which is Spirit. Of the twelve foundational apostles chosen by the Lord to lead His Church into the new age, not one of them was in a position of natural leadership. In fact, it seems that they were a unique fraternity of those voted "least likely to succeed".

The author of Hebrews explained because Israel did not know the ways of the Lord they were not able to enter His rest (Heb. 3:10-11). Because Israel was content only to see and be blessed — but were not concerned with knowing Him — it cost them their inheritance, just as it will us.

The land flowing with milk and honey and additional blessings the Lord wanted to give Israel were great — but they were not the reason the Lord brought them out of Egypt. Israel was called to be a nation of priests, to serve Him and manifest to all the peoples of the earth the character of their Creator (Ex. 19:5-6). But they didn't know Him! At Mount Sinai one of the most tragic events in Israel's history took place. It was there that the nation of Israel abdicated this high calling and decided they did not really want to know the Lord but would rather have a human mediator. This incident is recorded in Exodus 20:18-21.

> *And all the people perceived the thunder and the lightning flashes and the sound of the trumpet and the mountain smoking; and when the people saw it, they trembled and **stood at a distance**. Then they said to Moses, "**Speak to us yourself and we will listen; but let not God speak to us** lest we die". And Moses said to the people, "Do not be afraid; for God has come in order to test you, and in order that the fear of Him may remain with you, so that you may not sin." SO THE PEOPLE STOOD AT A DISTANCE, while Moses approached the thick cloud where God was.*

From this time on Israel had no desire for a personal relationship with the Lord. They wanted all the benefits but not Him. This has also been the history of the Christian church. The Church has proved willing to pay almost any price to have someone mediate its relationship with the Lord. This attitude has reduced the Church to a division — a cleavage which the Lord neither ordained nor recognized. Like Israel, the Church was called to be a kingdom of priests (Rev. 1:6). The propagation of a system that separated the priesthood from the congregation destroyed the very purpose of the Church.

"There is one God, and one mediator also between God and men, the man Christ Jesus" (1 Tim. 2:5). Whenever a man positions himself between the Lord and His people, he is usurping the position of the Lord Jesus Himself. Jesus alone can stand between God and man. There are apostles, prophets, evangelists, pastors and teachers, elders, deacons and other ministries that are given to the Church, but they are all given *"for the equipping of the saints for the work of service, to the building up of the body of Christ; until we all attain to the unity of the faith, and of the knowledge of the Son of God, to a mature man, to the measure of the stature which belongs to the fullness of Christ"* (Eph. 4:12-13).

No ministry is given to accomplish spiritual responsibilities for us. All ministry is given for the purpose of bringing the Church to maturity. We are all called as ministers; we are all called as priests. When any man is called *the* minister or *the* priest, he has usurped both the Lord's and the Church's authority. Each of us is a minister and priest.

That every man is called as a minister and a priest does not in any way negate the authority the Lord has established in the Church to keep order. Proper ministry could not occur without this authority. Even so, the authority is of a decreasing nature, not an increasing one. As the Church matures, these roles become unnecessary. Its ultimate purpose is to work itself out of a job, just as a parent's responsibility is to prepare the child for the day he is to leave the protection of the home and make his own way. The authority of the Church is given as protection for its spiritual children and to prepare them to stand on their own in Christ.

In Numbers 11:24-29, we see in Moses the spirit of proper ministry. The Lord had Moses gather the seventy elders to the tent of meeting so that He could ordain them to share Moses' responsibility and authority in the congregation. When the Spirit came upon them, they all began to prophesy. For an undisclosed reason two of the elders had remained in the camp, but the Spirit came upon them anyway and they prophesied in the camp. When a young man informed Moses of this, Joshua exhorted him to restrain them from prophesying. Moses replied, *"Are you jealous for my sake? I would that all of the Lord's people were prophets, that the Lord would put His Spirit upon them all!"* (verse 9). Moses was not threatened by possible encroachment — he knew there was more than enough for all to do! When one becomes protective of his spiritual domain, he has ceased to walk in true spiritual authority. It was Moses' delight to see other leaders raised up. It was not his desire to have Israel dependent upon him; and neither should we desire others to be dependent upon us. All true ministry is devoted to the end that people would individually come to know the Lord. Jesus demonstrated this same attitude: He explained to His disciples that it would be better for them if He went away so that they might receive the Spirit themselves.

The Commissioning to Ministry

All members of the body of Christ are called to be ministers. Everyone has a definite function that is essential to the Body as a whole. But just because we have been called to a ministry does not mean that we are ready for it. There may be many years between the time one perceives the calling and the time for the commission to begin. The time between the calling and the commissioning is an essential time of preparation. If we prematurely begin to walk in our ministries before being commissioned by the Holy Spirit, we are most likely hindering the fulfillment of that ministry. The will of man can never accomplish the purposes of God. It is not by might, nor by power nor the most noble human intentions — but only by His Spirit that the work of God is accomplished.

Each miracle of Jesus had profound significance. When He turned the water into wine, He was demonstrating His purposes for the disciples. The vessels were set aside and filled with water (water is often symbolic of the word of God {see Eph. 5:26}). This was the period of preparation in which they were to be "filled to the brim" with His teaching. After we have received God's calling, there must be a period of time in which we are set aside and filled. It is not enough to be partially filled; we must be completely full! It is not enough to be filled with just teaching either — the water must be turned into wine; our knowledge must become life. Only then are we ready to be poured out. Those who are poured out too soon seldom ever become "wine" (walk in the fullness of the anointing to which they have been called). The "water" they serve is refreshing and may bless many, but with patience the finest wine will be served. Those who have waited to become wine have shaken the world!

Moses is an excellent example of the Lord's preparation. He must have suspected a call to help the Israelites when he slew an Egyptian in their defense, but it was not God's time. He fled Egypt in seeming defeat. Then he spent forty years as a shepherd in the wilderness (the most humble profession of the times) before God ordained him for His work. It has been said that Satan builds a man up so that he can tear him down. The Lord tears a man down so that He can build him up! There are no short cuts to anointed ministry. Diplomas and titles may command the respect of men but they don't impress the Lord. Once we have tasted the wine of God, water will never satisfy.

The nature of the Lord is creative. No two people are alike and no two ministries are alike. Every prophet in the Bible is strikingly different, as are all the apostles. When the Lord calls us to specific ministry, we may be patterned after another ministry but only in a very general sense. Each of us is very different from anyone else ... in scripture, history, or among contemporaries. For this reason we cannot fashion ourselves into a ministry; only the Lord can do this. He is the one who is building His Church and fashioning each stone. We must allow the Lord to make us as He will. We must be willing to be very different from any others. Those who race off to fulfill their callings before the proper time inevitably become cheap imitations. Those that determine to be *different* and have not been shaped by God are even more pitiful.

Moses Strikes the Rock

In Numbers 20:8-12, we have a sobering example of one of the greatest snares to walking in spiritual power and authority. Moses was pressured greatly by people complaining of no water. The Lord commanded Moses to take his rod (a symbol of the authority the Lord had given Him) and *speak* to the rock to bring forth water. Instead of speaking to the rock, Moses struck it with his rod. Water came forth in abundance, but at grave cost. The Lord's discipline was most severe: *"But the Lord spoke to Moses and Aaron, 'Because you have not believed Me, to treat Me as holy in the sight of the sons of Israel, therefore you shall not bring this assembly into the Land which I have given them'"* (verse 12).

The authority the Lord gives us is awesome. Used in humility and submission, it is a powerful tool. Used presumptuously it can cost us our inheritance in Christ. The rock was Christ. The Lord's authority was not given so that we could strike Him with it . . . when we begin to demand compliance, we are actually commanding the Head to obey *us*. This is dangerous ground.

The body of Christ today is encouraged to search the scriptures for desired promises, hold those scriptures up to God and demand fulfillment. This could be the ultimate demonstration of the pride of man. This uses God's authority and principles for self-promotion! The Lord wants us to learn to use the rod — but for His purposes! When pride (self-centeredness) enters into spiritual authority, we are in danger. He is seeking those who *"tremble at His word"* to be His habitation (Is. 66:1-2). We must treat Him as holy or we, like Moses, may find ourselves banned from the promised land.

Fear of Man

The pressure of what people were saying spurred Moses to use his rod in a manner the Lord had not commanded. The same pressure has caused the downfall of many ministries. Humility is the fear of God, not man. *"By the fear of the Lord one keeps away from evil"* (Prov. 16:6). *"The fear of man brings a snare"* (Prov. 29:25). For this reason Paul declared, *"If I were still trying to please men, I would not be a bond-servant of Christ"* (Gal. 1:10). If we truly fear the Lord, we will not fear anyone else. To honor and respect the Lord for who He is is to be delivered from all fear of man.

Jesus declared to the Pharisees, *"You are those who justify yourselves in the sight of men, but God knows your hearts; for that which is highly esteemed in the sight of men is detestable in the sight of God"* (Luke 16:15). If we are compelled to seek the esteem of men, we will be found doing things which are detestable. We must determine who we are going to serve — man or God. We cannot please both. For this reason Jesus cautioned, *"Woe to you when all men speak well of you, for in the same way your fathers used to treat the false prophets"* (Luke 6:26). Our ministry will be false to the degree that it is affected by men.

We are called to be the servants of all men, but **men are not to be our masters.** We must be willing to give our lives for men but not be controlled or influenced by them. As the apostle exhorted, *"With good will render service, as to the Lord, and not to men"* (Eph. 6:7).

Possibly the greatest difference between King Saul and King David was who they wanted to please. Saul feared the people more than the Lord, whereas David feared the Lord more than the people. When Saul was commanded to wait until the prophet Samuel returned to make a sacrifice to the Lord before entering into battle, he would not wait because: *"I saw the people scattering from me . . . and the Philistines were gathering"* (1 Sam. 13:11). Anyone that has walked in leadership in the body of Christ understands the pressure which caused Saul to stumble. When the people begin to scatter and the enemy advances at the same time, the compulsion to do something is very great, even when the Lord has commanded us to wait. To give in to those pressures is to risk the anointing. God's anointing for leadership left Saul. If we are to function in true spiritual leadership, we must be in submission to God alone.

Compromise is also a deadly enemy . . . it is so easily justified in our minds. When Saul was later commanded to attack and utterly destroy the Amalekites, he attacked them, destroyed most of them, but kept alive the king and some of the best livestock. He justified keeping the animals by purposing to offer them to the Lord. The Amalekites are a type of Satanic force in scripture. During Israel's wilderness journey, the Amalekites attacked from the rear, picking off the weak and stragglers under cover of darkness. Sound like Satan? The Lord commanded that the Amalekites and all their possessions be destroyed as a type. During ancient times if one king defeated another in battle and kept him alive, he did so either to make him a slave or an ally. The Lord was instructing Saul by example that there can be absolutely no compromise in the destruction of Satan's territory. Saul rationalized that the king of the Amalekites could be made an ally or a servant. This is a dangerous assumption. He also reasoned he should keep the best of the Amalekites' possessions to sacrifice to the Lord. The things of Satan cannot be used in our worship of the Lord. Samuel's rebuke of Saul is a warning to us:

> *And Samuel said, "Has the Lord as much delight in burnt offerings and sacrifices as in obeying the voice of the Lord? Behold, to obey is better than sacrifice, and to heed than the fat of rams. For rebellion is as the sin of divination, and insubordination is as iniquity and idolatry"* (1 Sam. 15:22-23).

Sacrifice will never atone for rebellion. Many have fallen into the snare of believing good works can compensate for compromise or disobedience in other areas of our lives. This is the beginning of deception and divination (sorcery). We may think of sorcery as conjuring up spirits and spell-weaving, but these are simply extreme manifestations. Paul actually named sorcery as a work of the flesh (Gal. 5:20). Basically, sorcery (also called witchcraft) is using any spirit or device other than the Holy Spirit to dominate, control, or manipulate another person or situation. The subtle pressures we may exert to get our own way would fall into this category. Saul's sacrifices to the Lord as appeasements for his varied deviations are a good example of this. Imagine for a moment a little girl purring winningly to her father how much she loves him . . . right before he spanks her! In this situation this is done to manipulate her father, to atone for rebellion and hopefully avoid the spanking. If allowed to succeed, such devices will lead to more extreme practices in the future, just as Saul's failure to repent led him to destroy the Lord's priests and seek counsel from a sorcerer.

Saul confessed *"I have sinned; I have indeed transgressed the command of the Lord and your words, because I feared the people and listened to their voices"* (1 Sam. 15:24). Saul confessed his sin, and understood why he had sinned, **but he did not repent**. There is a difference between confession and repentance. Confession can actually be an attempt to manipulate, as in the case of Saul. In verse 30 the real reason for Saul's confession becomes clear: *"I have sinned; but please honor me now before the elders of my people and before Israel."* His confession was an attempt to induce Samuel to continue to honor him before the people. Had he truly repented, he would not have been concerned about what the people thought.

David was of a different spirit. Throughout the narrative of his life we read time after time *"David inquired of the Lord"*. Even when the Amalekites kidnapped his family and the families of his men and their possessions, with his own men threatening to stone him, David resisted taking action before seeking the Lord. The pressures of this situation must have been incredible. In a situation that would have caused even the strongest faith to doubt, of David it was said, *"But David strengthened himself in the Lord his God"*. David trusted in the Lord more than men or circumstances. This was the solid foundation upon which the throne of David was established. It was a foundation strong enough to endure forever. For any ministry to endure it must be built upon the same foundation.

The fear of man is a snare to any ministry. The Lord called Peter "Satan" because he set his mind on man's interests instead of God's (Matt. 16:23). James rebuked the church with a similar warning: *"You adulteresses, do you not know that friendship with the world is hostility toward God. Therefore whoever wishes to be a friend of the world makes himself an enemy of God"* (James 4:4). We are to love the world with Christ's love, but we are not to be its friend.

Compromising has robbed the Church of its power. When Moses went to Pharaoh to demand "Let my people go!", Pharaoh responded by increasing the burdens of Israel. The Lord responded by bringing plagues upon Egypt. After observing the power of God, Pharaoh tried to get Israel to compromise. He said that they could serve the Lord as long as they did it in Egypt (Ex. 8:25). When Satan sees that we are determined to serve the Lord, he will try to make us believe we can serve the Lord and still be of the world (Egypt is a type of the world, or present evil age). Moses did not give in. After greater demonstrations of the Lord's power, Pharaoh again proposed a compromise: *"I will let you go, that you may sacrifice to the Lord your God in the wilderness; only you shall not go far away"* (Ex. 8:28). Sound familiar? When one begins to break free of the world to serve the Lord, he hears from a multitude of sources the dangers of going too far with religion. True believers refuse to let the world dictate how far they will go with the Lord.

After even greater demonstrations of the Lord's power, Pharaoh again proposed a compromise: *"Go serve the Lord* (no prerequisites on how far they can go now); *only let your flocks and your herds be detained. Even your little ones may go with you"* (Ex. 10:24). Satan's last attempt at getting us to compromise is to have us leave something in "Egypt" because he knows where your treasure is there will your heart be also. We too must declare, as Moses did, *"not a hoof will be left behind".*

Pharaoh's strategy to keep Israel in bondage is a parallel of the strategy which Satan still uses to keep men under his control and away from the cross. As soon as Moses proclaimed liberty to Israel by the word of the Lord, Pharaoh countered by giving his men instructions to: *"Let the labor be heavier on the men, and let them work at it that they may pay no attention to false words"* (Ex. 5:9). Pharaoh's strategy was to make the burdens on God's people heavier so that they would think that God's promises were "false words". Satan does the same to us; just before we are about to be delivered by the power of God he heaps the burdens on us to make us think that God's word is false.

This strategy against Israel began to work, causing them to doubt and become discouraged. To bring *DISCOURAGEMENT* is Satan's first priority. If we are not ignorant of the enemy's schemes, we will be prepared for them and can combat them just as Moses did. If God gives you a promise, for example one of healing, Satan will immediately try to make you feel worse, thus getting you to turn from the promise of God as being false. We must learn to expect this attack when we receive the promise of God and not allow it to discourage us into thinking that His word is false.

After Moses and the people remained determined, Satan's next strategy was to duplicate the miracles of God. If the first tactic does not work, Satan will then try to make us think that there really is not anything special or unique about what God is promising or that God's power is no greater than his. This is meant to bring disorientation. *DISORIENTATION* will be Satan's next tactic after he has been successful in sowing discouragement.

Because Moses remained determined, Pharaoh's next tactic was more cunning: he told them to *"Go sacrifice to your God within the land"* (Ex. 8:25). When Satan sees that we are determined to serve the Lord, he will then try to make us think that we can serve God even though we remain under his bondage to the ways of this world. This is likened to the delusion that we can still maintain our former sins, but be forgiven as long as we go to church occasionally or say that we are believers. Moses was not deceived, and neither must we be by this fallacy. After *DISCOURAGEMENT* and *DISORIENTA-TION*, Satan's next weapon will be *COMPROMISE*.

When this tactic failed, Pharaoh's next strategy was to allow them to go but to get them to agree not to go very far. *"I will let you go, that you may sacrifice to the Lord your God in the wilderness; only you shall not go far away"* (Ex. 8:28). This was Satan's attempt to get Israel to *LOSE HER VISION* for the Promised Land. This strategy has been most effective on many Christians. When we lose our vision, we will just wander in the wilderness, making us easy prey for recapture. The call on Israel was not just to leave Egypt, but to go to the Promised Land. We must keep our vision on the ultimate purpose of God or we will be distracted by a lesser purpose.

When Moses remained steadfast to the call and vision of God, Pharaoh gave in a little but tried once more to get any measure of compromise that he could. He knew that if they compromised to any degree, he would regain dominion over them. He told them that they could go as far away as they wanted and he only had one condition: *"Only let your flocks and your herds be detained. Even your little ones can go with you"* (Ex. 10:24). This was another deadly diabolical trick. When Satan sees that we are utterly determined to "go all the way with Jesus", he then tries to get us to leave something behind. Satan understands very well that "Where your treasure is there will your heart be also". Compromise is spelled D-E-F-E-A-T for the people of God. We must be unrelenting in our determination to be utterly free of Satan's dominion over us or anything that is ours, responding like Moses, *"Therefore, our livestock, too, will go with us; not a hoof will be left behind!"* (Ex. 10:26).

In this scenario between Moses and Pharaoh, we have a lucid example of Satan's ancient strategy to keep God's people under his dominion. His first goal is to cause *DEPRESSION*, which leads to *DISORIENTATION*, then *LOSS OF VISION*, which leads to *COMPROMISE*, which brings to *DEFEAT* to the purpose of God for His people.

Even with Pharaoh's defeat in implementing this strategy, he did not give up, and we should never expect Satan to release us of his own free will. Israel was not to be freed by the dictate of Pharaoh, lest he say that he had let them go. Israel was only to be freed by the power of God. His power would bring destruction to the whole dominion of Pharaoh and give the treasures of Egypt into the hand of His people. We too must understand that we are not set free by the permission of Satan or by our own steadfastness, but by the power of God. We too will spoil Satan's dominion when we uncompromisingly partake of the true Passover sacrifice of the Lamb.

Let us make straight paths for our feet, not turning to the right or to the left, and not compromising regardless of how reasonable the proposition may seem. In this way we will remain in the place where the power of the cross can work to bring us release, as well as bring judgement upon the dominion of the evil one.

7

The Passover

Christ our Passover also has been sacrificed (1 Cor. 5:7).

It was the Passover sacrifice which delivered Israel from the power of Pharaoh so that her people would never again serve Egypt. It is the cross, of which the Passover was a prophetic type, that delivers us from the power of Satan and slavery to the corruption of the world. Realizing this, Satan rages against those who turn to the cross just as Pharaoh did against Israel when he saw that he was losing his power over them. Like the Passover did in type, the cross brings judgement upon the evil of the world, but delivers those who embrace it from the world.

Since Cain and Abel, the sacrifice has been the main point of conflict between the two seeds, which represent the two natures of man — carnal and spiritual. Satan is not threatened if we embrace the doctrines or the institution of Christianity; in fact he may well encourage it. He knows that the good of the Tree of Knowledge is just as deadly as the evil and far more deceptive. Human goodness is an affront to the cross and is used as a compensation for it. It deludes us into thinking that if we do more "good" than evil, we will be acceptable to the Father, thereby placing us above the need for the sacrifice of His Son. Satan may well encourage us to embrace anything religious as long as we do not turn to the cross. When we turn to the cross, Satan's power over us is completely broken; at that point we march out of his dominion into the glorious liberty of the Spirit — a relationship with our God.

The greatest opposition to one embracing the cross and the true liberty of the Spirit will be religious man. This battle began with the first two brothers, Cain and Abel, and rages to this day. The cross will always be the greatest threat to religious man, and religious man will always be the greatest enemy of the cross. It was not the demon possessed who persecuted Jesus; they bowed the knee and submitted to Him. It was the religious, moral and conservative citizens who crucified Jesus, and these will be the ones to rise up against anyone who preaches the true message of the cross. The greatest persecution against the true faith will always come from those who have been converted in their minds but not in their hearts. These will be those who in fact live by the fruit of the Tree of The Knowledge of Good and Evil instead of the fruit of the Tree of Life. Their true devotion will be to intellectual comprehension of doctrines in place of a living relationship with God and compliance with His *will*.

As Jesus warned, *"Not every one who says to Me, Lord, Lord, will enter the kingdom of heaven; but he who does the will of My Father who is in heaven."* (Matt. 7:21). We will only know true doctrine if we esteem doing His will *above* just knowing the doctrine, as He further explained: *"If any man is willing to do His will, he shall know of the doctrine, whether it is of God, or whether I speak from myself"* (John 7:17).

A person can desire truth for many different reasons, some of which are evil such as pride, self-justification or even fear. It is only those who have a love for the truth who will not be deceived in the evil day. Those who love the truth do want their doctrines to be accurate and pure. We will only have accurate and pure doctrines if we love the God of Truth more than the truths of God. It is not knowing the book of the Lord that gives life, but knowing the Lord of the book. If we love the Truth Himself more than we love the individual truths, we will love those truths more than we would if we esteemed them more than we do Him. It is not a matter of having one or the other but having both if we have them in the proper order.

A New Beginning

Now the Lord said to Moses and Aaron in the land of Egypt, "This month shall be the beginning of months to you; it is to be the first month of the year to you" (Ex. 12:1-2).

As the Passover was to be the archetypical prophecy of the sacrifice of Jesus, it is significant to note that Moses prepared Israel for the first Passover by rotating its calendar to a "first month". This heralded a new beginning. After partaking of the Passover, the children of Israel were to leave the only place they had ever known, to travel through lands they had never seen, to possess a land about which they had only dreamed. Their life would never be the same after that one fateful day — and neither is ours.

Therefore if any man be in Christ, he is a new creature: old things are passed away; behold all things are become new (2 Cor. 5:17, KJV).

When Jesus becomes our Passover, we are born again into a new world. To Israel it was a physical change; to us it is a spiritual change. The external conditions and surroundings may remain the same, but we do not. The externals appear different, but it is because our eyes are new! When one is born again, he begins to see the Kingdom of God (John 3:3). This is a far more glorious deliverance. Moses led Israel out of Egypt in one day, but "Egypt" (the ways of the world) still remains in Israel. Through Christ *"the world has been crucified to me, and I to the world"* (Gal. 6:14). Jesus takes Egypt out of the heart and replaces it with a new country — the Kingdom of God. The seed of Cain, religious man, is forever seeking to make the world a better place in which to live. Christ changes men so that they might be better able to live in the world. The carnal man seeks to change men by changing the world. The spiritual man seeks to change the world by changing men.

Except for this tiny little pocket of darkness called earth, the glory of God prevails over the universe. Even through we are but a speck in the great expanse of creation, the Father made the supreme sacrifice to redeem and restore us by sending His own Son, to the overwhelming wonder of creation. But for this awesome fact, earth would register "zero" in significance compared to the expanse of God's dominion. When we begin to perceive the Lord and the dimensions of His dominion, personal and even world problems begin to look insignificant. We can be sure that this one drop of evil will never overcome the oceans of His goodness. His kingdom will come! It is an irresistible force that will overshadow evil just as the sun overshadows the moon when it rises.

When man ate of the Tree of Knowledge, his attention became focused upon himself and he began to think of himself as the center of the universe. Every child born after the fall inherited this deception. Our little problems and ambitions completely dominate our minds until we are converted. Then, as we begin to see the Kingdom of God, our perspective is changed. The more clearly we see Him sitting on His throne, the less we notice the combined problems and cares of the world. Not that we do not care about them — we simply realize that He is so much bigger than any problem and more wonderful than any human ambition! As we see Him with new eyes, we find a peace that is beyond comprehension. The world may not be one bit different, but we are.

Walking in truth is walking with God. As our vision of His kingdom is clarified, the things of earth do grow dim. The things that are invisible to the natural man become more real to us than things that are seen. To those who do not see in the spirit, this sounds absurd. The apostle Paul explained it well:

But a natural man does not accept the things of the Spirit of God; for they are foolishness to him, and he cannot understand them, because they are spiritually appraised.

But he who is spiritual appraises all things (accurately), *yet he himself is appraised by no man* (1 Cor. 2:14-15).

If we were to wake up and see Jesus standing beside our bed, physically manifested, the day at the office would be quite different! How would the day change if He were to visibly accompany us to the office? To those born of the Spirit, "the eyes of the heart" see more clearly than the natural eyes. The Lord is with us wherever we go because He lives in us. When the eyes of our hearts remain open, we will be beholding Him continually. That is reality — seeing Jesus in the power of His resurrection as the King over all rulers, powers and authorities.

When Stephen was martyred, he was not even distracted by the stones that were killing him. He was looking at Jesus! The apostle

Paul, who was yet unconverted, witnessed the reality of Stephen's vision as he was being stoned. The Lord was even then preparing His chosen vessel to carry His name before the Gentiles, kings and the sons of Israel. The seed that was planted in Paul's heart when he saw the reality Stephen lived in was to bear much fruit. Years later he wrote these penetrating verses about having the vision for this reality:

> *I pray that the eyes of your heart may be enlightened, so that you may know what is the hope of His calling, what are the riches of the glory of His inheritance in the saints,*
>
> *and what is the surpassing greatness of His power toward us who believe. These are in accordance with the working of the strength of His might*
>
> *which He brought about in Christ, when He raised Him from the dead, and seated Him at the right hand in the heavenly places,*
>
> *far above all rule and authority and power and dominion, and every name that is named, not only in this age, but also the age to come.*
>
> *And He put all things in subjection under His feet, and gave Him as head over all things to the church, which is His body, the fullness of Him who fills all in all* (Eph. 1:18-23).

When Paul perceived Jesus on His throne, he saw all things subjected to Him. Jesus is still on the throne. *All* dominion has been given to Him and nothing can happen that He does not allow. It is impossible for Satan to sneak in a blow when Jesus is not looking. When the eyes of our heart are opened to see this, it is difficult to give much credence to the cares of the world. Elisha was another who had this vision. When confronted by an entire army, he sat peacefully on the side of a hill, much to his servant's dismay. When Elisha prayed for the servant's eyes to be opened, the servant was then able to understand the reason for Elisha's confidence: the angels standing for them outnumbered the enemy (see 2 Kings 6:8-23).

Walking in the Spirit is to see with His eyes, hear with His ears, and understand with His heart. As we do this, the earth with all of its problems and its glories starts to appear as small as it really is in the realm of the Spirit. After we have beheld the glory and authority of Jesus, kings and presidents are no more impressive than the wretched. Once we have seen the Lord, all earthly pomp and position appears ludicrous, and the worst international crisis is hardly cause for concern. The King is on His throne, and He will never lose control.

When Isaiah saw the Lord sitting on His throne, there were seraphim with Him who called out to one another: *"Holy, holy, holy, is the Lord of Hosts, the whole earth is full of His glory"* (Is. 6:3). With all of the wars, conflicts, disasters, diseases, and confusion, how can the seraphim say that the whole earth is full of His glory? They are able to say it because they dwell in the presence of the Lord. As we begin to dwell in His presence, we too will see the whole earth as being full of His glory, regardless of the circumstances. We see the realities of what is taking place on earth, but we also see the greater reality of God's plan and power. We are citizens of the new creation, not the old, and we must see from the perspective of the new.

Now we might ask why we have this continual battle with our old nature if we are new creatures. We would not have this battle if we kept our eyes on Jesus. It is when we, like Peter, take our eyes off Him and focus on the tossing waves of the world and the flesh that we begin to sink. As Paul explained to the Romans:

> *For I know that nothing good dwells in me, that is, in my flesh; for the wishing is present in me, but the doing of good is not.*
>
> *For the good that I wish, I do not do; but I practice the very evil that I do not wish.*
>
> *But if I am doing the very thing I do not wish, I am no longer the one doing it, but sin which dwells in me.*

I find then the principle that evil is present in me, the one who wishes to do good.

For I joyfully concur with the law of God in the inner man,

but I see a different law in the members of my body, waging war against the law of my mind, and making me a prisoner of the law of sin which is in my members.

Wretched man that I am! Who will set me free from this body of death? **Thanks be to God through Christ Jesus our Lord** (Rom. 7:18-25).

Without Christ, there is no good thing in us. No matter how many times we look at ourselves, we will find the same thing — evil. But in Christ we no longer have to live by our sinful nature! He has given us His Life, His Spirit! When He said, *"It is finished"*, He meant it. He is the finished work of God; He is the finished work the Father seeks to accomplish in us. Maturity is not accomplished by striving to reach a certain level of spirituality; maturity is simply abiding in Him Who is the finished work of God. Jesus *is* our wisdom, righteousness, sanctification and redemption (1 Cor. 1:30). Jesus is everything we are called to be; we can only be that which we have been called to be by abiding in Him.

We will never become the new creation we are called to be by setting spiritual goals and attaining them. We can only attain true spirituality by abiding in the One who *is* the work of God. Jesus is the Alpha and Omega, the Beginning and the End of all things. Jesus is called "the firstborn of all creation" (Col. 1:15). Jesus is the whole Purpose of God. Everything that the Father loved and esteemed He brought forth in His Son. Everything was created *by* Him and *for* Him and in Him all things hold together (Col. 1:16-17). The whole creation was *for* the Son. All things are to be summed up in Him (Eph. 1:10). We accomplish the whole purpose of God in our life when we have our whole being summed up in Him by simply abiding in Him.

See to it that no one takes you captive through philosophy and empty deception, according to the tradition of men, according to the elementary principles of the world, rather than according to Christ.

For in Him all the fulness of the Deity dwells in bodily form,

and in Him you have been made complete (Col. 2:8-10)

We can, in our own strength, change our outward behavior to some degree, but only the Lord can change our hearts. We cannot even judge the thoughts and intentions of our hearts accurately, *"For the heart is more deceitful than all else and is desperately sick; who can understand it?"* (Jer. 17:9). We may have pretty good motives one day and terrible ones the next. If we only do things when our motives are right, we will easily be foiled by Satan or deceived by our own hearts, even while we may have the best of intentions. If we allow our motives to control us, we will be in perpetual confusion. Our lives must be determined by the will of God, not our motives. Paul explained this to the Corinthians:

But to me it is a very small thing that I should be examined by you, or by any human court; in fact, I do not even examine myself.

I am conscious of nothing against myself, yet I am not by this acquitted; but the one who examines me is the Lord (1 Cor. 4:3-4).

This does not mean that we ignore our problems, but we must depend upon the Lord's word to divide between soul and spirit. We are to "judge ourselves lest we be judged", but this must be done by the Spirit. Our judgement of ourselves can be distorted if it is not done by the Spirit. Our hearts are deceitful, and often we are more easily deceived by our own hearts than others are. We must depend on the Lord to change us if the change is to be real. We are changed as we behold His glory, not our own failings (2 Cor. 3:18).

But let us not be presumptuous; this does not give us license to follow evil motives. We are only to disregard our motives when they are in conflict with the will of God, not to pursue our own ends. Through Jesus, *"He condemned sin in the flesh"* (Rom. 8:3). It is false doctrine which teaches God's grace as continual forgiveness for continual sin. When we abuse His grace and live after the flesh, we have departed from grace.

He promised that we will never be tempted beyond what we are able to endure (1 Cor. 10:13). The grace that the Lord has given us is the **power** to walk by His Spirit. As Peter stated: *"Seeing that His divine power has granted (past tense) to us everything pertaining to life and godliness (God-likeness), through the true knowledge of Him"* (2 Pet. 1:3).

When we give in to the flesh, it is not because we do not have the strength to resist — we are simply giving in to sin! It's like training for a marathon. When the runner thinks he cannot go another step, if he will relax he will find that he can go a great deal further, and his endurance increases from that point. When we get to the point where we don't think we can stand the temptation any longer, if we will just rest in Him who has conquered all sin, we can endure far past the point at which we usually give up. It is at the point that we cannot stand it any longer that His strength takes over. *"My grace is sufficient for you, for My power is perfected in weakness"* (2 Cor. 12:9).

Therefore, do not throw away your confidence, which has a great reward.

For you have need of endurance, so that when you have done the will of God, you may receive what was promised.

For yet in a little while, He who is coming will come, and will not delay.

But My righteous one shall live by faith; and if he shrinks back, My soul has no pleasure in him.

But we are not of those who shrink back to destruction, but of those who have faith to the preserving of the soul (Heb. 10:35-39).

The athlete's endurance does not increase until he reaches the previous limit of his endurance and overtakes it. The same is true of our spiritual endurance. We can testify with Paul: *"I can do all things through Him who strengthens me"* (Phil. 4:13). In Christ we can never say "can't" to what He has called us to do. We can say we that we "will not" or "did not", but we can never say that we "can not". He has given us *His* strength.

> *In Him you were circumcised with a circumcision made without hands, in the removal of the body of the flesh by the circumcision of Christ* (Col. 2:11).

> *There is therefore now no condemnation for those who are in Christ Jesus. For the law of the Spirit of life in Christ Jesus has set you free from the law of sin and death. For what the Law could not do, weak as it was through the flesh and as an offering for sin, He condemned sin in the flesh* (Rom. 8:1-3).

The Lord is not just trying to change us; He is trying to *kill* us! The ultimate high calling of God is attained when we can say with the apostle, *"I have been crucified with Christ; and it is no longer I who live, but Christ lives in me; and the life which I now live in the flesh I live by faith in the Son of God, who loved me and delivered Himself up for me"* (Gal. 2:20).

John the Baptist was a wonderful type of true spiritual ministry. His whole purpose and devotion was to prepare the way for Jesus, to point to Him, and then to decrease as He increased. He did not say that he would decrease *so that* Jesus could increase, but he said Jesus *"must increase, but I must decrease"* (John 3:30). If we try to decrease *so* Jesus can increase we are still pursuing a self-righteousness by which we try to dictate His increase. Again, it is as we see Him and His glory that we are changed into His same image (2 Cor. 3:18). Only then will there be a true decrease of our own self-life. To presume that we can crucify our own flesh is vanity. If we were to crucify ourselves, all that we would have left is self-righteousness. We do not crucify ourselves, but rather we are crucified *"with Christ"*.

The new birth is possibly the greatest demonstration of the love and grace of God. We have all sinned and are worthy of eternal destruction. But the Father so loved us that He sent His own Son to be a propitiation for our sins, allowing us to start all over again.

We exchange our body of death for eternal life as the Lord's own children. No genius of fantasy or fiction could have ever dreamed a more wonderful story. How could we who have partaken of such glory not *"do all things for the sake of the gospel"* (1 Cor. 9:23)?

> *For the love of Christ controls us, having concluded this, that one died for all, therefore all died;*
>
> *and He died for all, that they who live should no longer live for themselves, but for Him, who died and rose again on their behalf.*
>
> *Therefore from now on we recognize no man according to the flesh; even though we have known Christ according to the flesh, yet we know Him thus no longer.*
>
> *Therefore if any man is in Christ, he is a new creature; the old things passed away; behold new things have come.*
>
> *Now all these things are from God, who reconciled us to Himself through Christ, and gave us the ministry of reconciliation,*
>
> *namely, that God was in Christ reconciling the world to Himself, not counting their trespasses against them, and He has committed to us the word of reconciliation.*
>
> *Therefore, we are ambassadors for Christ, as though God were entreating through us; we beg you on behalf of Christ, be reconciled to God.*
>
> *He made Him who knew no sin to be sin on our behalf, that we might be the righteousness of God in Him.* (2 Cor. 5:14-21)

Taking the Lamb into the House

> *Speak to all the congregation of Israel, saying, "On the tenth of this month they are each one to take a lamb for themselves,*

according to their father's households, a lamb for each house-
hold. And you shall keep it until the fourteenth day of the same
month" (Ex. 12:3,6).

The purpose of taking the lamb into the house five days before
the sacrifice was to carefully examine it for flaws. This was a
prophecy that Jesus, the true Passover Lamb, would enter Jerusalem
five days before His crucifixion. He did this, perfectly fulfilling the
Word. While He was entering the city, the ritual Passover lambs
were themselves being taken into the houses. As these lambs were
being examined for disqualifying flaws, the scribes, Pharisees, and
Sadducees were challenging Jesus trying to find a flaw in Him. None
was found; He was the acceptable sacrifice for God's Passover. The
rulers finally resigned themselves to hiring false witnesses against
Him.

In John 19:42, we note that Jesus was slain on the Jewish Day of
Preparation. On this day all the Passover lambs were slain to
prepare for the feast. As Jesus was nailed to the cross, knives were
being put to the throats of sacrificial lambs throughout Israel. The
fulfillment of the type was taking place right in their midst.

Even His own disciples did not understand what was happening.
Do we yet understand what has happened? Jesus alone is the Lamb
who is without blemish. We may know this in our minds, but do we
yet believe it in our hearts? How is it that we still judge our ability
to be accepted by the Father by how well we are doing, instead of
the *only* way that we have become acceptable to Him, by the blood
of His Son? Our ability to come boldly before the throne of grace
must never be measured by how good or bad we have been, but by
the blood of Jesus; any other motive is an affront to that cross.

If we are being obedient in order to become acceptable, we are
being an affront to the cross which alone has gained our approval
with God. True ministry does not come in order to gain God's
approval, but it comes from a position of *having* His approval
because of the Lamb. We are obedient because we have been
bought with a price and we no longer belong to ourselves but to
Him who has purchased us with His own life. We love Him because
He first loved us. We now labor because we love Him for *the price*
He paid to gain our acceptance, and we long to see Him receive the
reward of His sacrifice. There is a difference between trying to

please God because we love Him and want to bring Him joy and trying to please Him in order to be acceptable. The former is worship; the latter is still the self-seeking pursuit of self-righteousness.

Our failure to understand this aspect of the Passover may well be an answer to why there has been such a superficial nature to modern conversions. Major, international evangelists confess that less than twenty percent of those who make a decision in their crusades go on to walk with the Lord. Could it be that there is something lacking in the gospel we preach? Could it be that instead of trying to get such hasty "decisions" we would serve men better if, like Israel, we encouraged them to take the Lamb into their "houses" for a few days before they embrace the sacrifice? Would the decisions not be more real if men were encouraged to first examine Jesus thoroughly so that they would know for themselves that there is no flaw in Him?

There are times when a person is ready to make a decision and be reborn immediately. But generally, some of our modern evangelistic methods are not bearing fruit that remains. In the parable of the sower, the Lord said that, *"When anyone hears the word of the kingdom, and does not understand it, the evil one comes along and snatches away what has been sown in his heart"* (Matt. 13:19). Likewise, He said, *"The one on whom the seed was sown on the good soil, this is the man who hears the word and understands it"* (verse 23).

There are times when we need to heed the biblical exhortation to not lean on our own understanding (Prov. 3:5), but not at conversion. Those who make a commitment because of hype, emotional stimulation, or even at the prompting of anointed preaching are in danger of having the seed snatched away if they do not understand it. If one is inclined to trust an issue as significant as eternal life to something he does not understand, is it even possible that he has believed in his heart?

As precious as redemption, salvation and the purposes of God are, one who has truly believed in his heart will be compelled to sink his roots as deep as possible into these matters. True faith is not blind; it is illumination in the most profound sense. True faith has nothing to fear from examination; it has everything to gain. There is a difference between believing in the mind and believing in the heart, but they are not mutually exclusive. If we are truly examining Jesus, not just intellectual concepts, the more closely we look at Him the more our hearts will be stirred to believe. Even Napoleon, after reading the gospel of John, stated that if Jesus was not the Son of God then the one who wrote that gospel was!

There was a time when Jesus asked His disciples who men said that He was. They answered *"Some say John the Baptist; some, Elijah, and others Jeremiah, or one of the prophets"* (Matt. 16:14). He then challenged them with the question *"But who do you say that I am?"* (verse 15). If they were to be true disciples, they could not be following Him because of who others said He was. The same is true with us. It is not who our pastor says He is or our favorite author, teacher or televangelist. Sooner or later that finger has got to be pointed right in our own chest — "Who do *you* say that the Son of Man is?"! We cannot be converted to another man's Jesus; He has got to be *our* Jesus.

When Peter answered the Lord's question that He was the Christ, the Son of God, the Lord replied, *"Blessed are you, Simon Barjona, because flesh and blood did not reveal this to you, but My Father who is in heaven"* (verse 17). Peter was obviously not moved by what others thought of Jesus; he was open to receive his own revelation. When we are open to receiving our own revelation from the Father, like Peter we are building upon a rock that the gates of hell cannot prevail against. One can teach a parrot to say the right things and do the right things, but it will never be in it's heart. If our understanding is simply the parroting of another, it is not true understanding, it is not in our heart, and it will never stand the test which surely comes upon every seed that is planted.

This is not meant to be an attack upon particular evangelist's methods. Like Paul, we should rejoice that Jesus is being preached even if the results are not perfect. Even if just twenty percent are converted, that is still a great many who may not have been reached had these men not been out there doing what they were doing. But there is wisdom in the biblical pattern of having those who would partake of the Passover sacrifice examine the Lamb thoroughly before doing so. We will not lose any true converts by doing this; we may gain many.

He Was Crucified By Us All

The whole assembly of the congregation of Israel is to kill it (the lamb) at twilight (Ex. 12:6).

And all the people answered and said, "His blood be on us and on our children" (Matt. 27:25).

As prophesied, it was the whole congregation of Israel that delivered Jesus to be crucified. Yet it was not just Israel that crucified Him; it was the carnal nature of man that is within us all. Had the Lord chosen to send His son to any other nation, there would have been the same results. Even Plato perceived that a truly righteous man would be despised by all men and eventually be impaled (the Greek equivalent of crucifixion). True Christians have always been persecuted and are still persecuted in almost every nation of the world. The Lord Himself declared, *"As you have done unto the least of these brothers of Mine you have done it unto Me"* (Matt. 25:40). Jesus has completely identified Himself with those for whom He died. If we have ever persecuted, slandered, or brought injury upon any of His, we have done it to the Lord himself. If we have betrayed a congregation, a minister, or a brother — even one who is the least, even one who is in doctrinal error or has other problems — we have betrayed the Lord Himself.

Let us not continue casting stones at others who fall short of God's glory because we have also fallen. When we judge another servant, or congregation of the Lord, we are in fact judging Him. What we are saying when we judge another one of God's sheep is that His workmanship does not meet up to our standards, and that we could do it better.

When the people rose up against Moses, his reply was that they were not rebelling against him but against God (Ex. 16:8). Moses did not mean by this that he was perfect or that everything he did was perfect, but that he was the one God had appointed as the leader. If Israel rebelled against Moses, they were saying that God did not know what He was doing by appointing him.

The same may be true of our tendency to judge leaders or even circumstances. If we are critical of a person or the circumstance the Lord has us in, we are in fact saying that we do not think the Lord knows what He is doing in ordering our life. We are not just judging the circumstance, we are judging God. The same may be true if we are judging our spouses, families, or superiors. How can we trust the Lord with our eternal salvation if we can not trust Him in the everyday matters of life? Of course, there are cases where we are in the wrong job or other circumstance. Then we should be preparing for a change, not by being critical, but with faith and a joyful heart, praying for the situation or people we are leaving.

Let us never be so foolish as to be critical of God and His workmanship. It was because of their **grumbling** and **complaining** that the first generation to leave Egypt perished in the wilderness. It is for the same reason that many of us never leave the wilderness where we have been placed for temporary training. If we lack faith like Israel in the wilderness, we go around and around the same mountain of trial; only when we begin to believe God will we be able to leave.

Possibly the greatest reason for the church's lack of light, power and a closer relationship with the Lord is her critical spirit. The Lord directly addressed this through the prophet Isaiah:

Then your light will break out like the dawn, and your recovery will speedily spring forth; and your righteousness will go before you; the glory of the Lord will be your rear guard.

Then you will call, and the Lord will answer; you will cry, and He will say "Here I am." IF you remove the yoke for your midst, the pointing of the finger, and speaking wickedness. (Is. 58:8-9)

The Lord here promises light, restoration, righteousness, the glory of the Lord and answered prayer if we remove the yoke of the critical spirit (pointing of the finger and speaking wickedness). As if we needed even more motivation than this to repent of this evil, Jesus gave it to us:

Do not judge lest you be judged.

For in the way you judge, you will be judged; and by your standard of measure, it shall be measured to you. (Matt. 7:1-2)

We have seen this so often fulfilled. Those who set themselves up as judges to criticize others with different views or doctrines end up becoming stumbling blocks, doing more damage to the church in the name of truth than many do with error. A stumbling block is the very last thing one would want to be as the Lord warned:

> *It is inevitable that stumbling blocks come; but woe to him through whom they come!*

> *It would be better for him if a millstone were hung around his neck and he were thrown into the sea, that he should cause one of these little ones to stumble.* (Luke 17:1-2)

In addressing the Corinthian problem of immorality, Paul asked *"Do you not judge those who are within the church?"* (1 Cor. 5:12). Those in leadership do have the authority and the responsibility to judge those who are within the church, but there is a certain biblical pattern which must be followed. This judgement can almost always be distinguished from that which is coming from stumbling blocks by how it complies with the biblical wisdom for judging within the church. First we are commanded to go to the person we believe is in sin or error alone. *If* the person does not repent, we are then to take another with us to entreat him further. Only if the person fails to repent after this is it lawful to bring the issue before the church (see Matt. 18:15-17).

The Lord's command as to the manner in which we are to reprove those who are in error was given immediately following His exhortation about the stumbling blocks. Those who go public with their accusations without complying to this mandate have almost certainly placed themselves in jeopardy of being stumbling blocks, regardless of how accurate their judgement is.

Even if we comply with the Lord's mandate in this, we can still be in error if we do it in the wrong spirit as Paul warned the Galatians:

> *Brethren, even if a man is caught in **any** trespass, you who are spiritual, restore such a one in a spirit of gentleness; looking to yourself, lest you too be tempted.* (Gal. 6:1)

It is no accident that those who go public with their judgement of others end up falling publicly. Those who write books in the spirit of the "accuser of the brethren" are soon consumed with spiritual paranoia and darkness of heart. The repercussions for speaking in a critical spirit about a brother are bad in this life but even more terrible when we stand before the Lord's judgement seat. Those who measure out judgement will have it measured back to them in the same measure. Those who show mercy will receive mercy; those who give grace will have the same. As we are all in desperate need of mercy and grace, let us be devoted to being vessels for the same.

But I say to you that every one who is angry with his brother shall be guilty before the court; and whoever shall say to his brother, "Raca," shall be guilty before the supreme court; and whoever shall say, "You Fool," shall be guilty enough to go into the fiery hell.

If therefore you are presenting your offering at the altar, and there remember that your brother has something against you,

leave your offering there before the altar, and go your way; first be reconciled to your brother, and then come and present your offering. (Matt. 5:22-24)

Some have misconstrued this text to justify going to a brother that they have something against, but that is not what it is saying. We are compelled to forgive those who may have wronged us, but we are asked to go and make right what someone may have against us. In this we are commanded to show mercy, *but not expect or require it from others*. What they do in this is between them and the Lord; we are to be concerned only with ourselves. This may seem unfair, but the Lord does not mean for it to be fair. If we want what is fair, we have all sinned and are worthy of death! Every chance we have to forgive and show mercy or grace is a great opportunity to receive more mercy and grace from the Lord. But when we show mercy or forgive, let us do it secretly before the Father that He may reward us. When we do this in a way so as to receive recognition, we have received our reward by that recognition.

There was a wonderful story related about a South Pacific culture where it was the custom of men to trade cows for a wife. A father might receive two cows for an average daughter. An above average girl would usually bring her father three cows. Only a rare beauty would ever bring four cows. There was a father here with a daughter so homely that he was hoping he could get even one cow for her. There was another man on the island who was considered their most astute trader. To everyone's astonishment, this man came and offered eight cows for this father's homely daughter! Everyone thought the wise trader had lost his mind, but it was not long before this homely girl was transformed into the most beautiful and gracious woman in the land. She had started to think of herself as an eight cow woman, and she became one!

We determine the value of a commodity by what someone is willing to pay for it. What were we bought with? What was our wife, husband, child, parent, friend or boss bought with? The most precious commodity in all of creation was paid for them — the blood of the Son of God. We must begin knowing one another after the Spirit, and seeing each other as God does. When we do this we will begin to see as dramatic a change in some as there was in the homely young girl from the South Pacific. We must stop crucifying the Lord again in each other, but begin esteeming the Lord and His workmanship in each one, giving the value to one another which He gave. Few things will work to the edification of the whole body of Christ so much as our starting to know each other after the Spirit instead of after the flesh. Let us pray to only see with His eyes, hear with His ears and understand with His heart. Then we will be the most astute and wise men in the land.

*Therefore, thus says the Lord, "If you return, then I will restore you — before Me you will stand. **And if you extract the precious from the worthless, you will become My spokesman**"* (Jer. 15:19).

When we start to see the precious in that which appears worthless and begin speaking to it and drawing it out of one another, we will start to become the prophetic people we must be to accomplish the mandate of God for this hour. Let us stop crucifying Christ again when He comes in even the least of His little ones but start recognizing Him, honoring Him and calling Him forth in one another.

Like the Pharisees in the first century, many Christians are usually looking for Jesus on His white horse, conquering and reigning, even when they are looking for Him in His people. This is truly His state in heaven, but if we want to see Jesus in His people, we sometimes have to have the heart of Simeon and Anna. They were able to see in a mere infant the Salvation of the whole world. We are sometimes so busy looking for the fruit we fail to see the seed that is to become the fruit. Let us be discerning enough not to miss Him in whatever form He appears. True wise men will worship Him even in His infancy. True apostles are yet in labor that He might be formed in His people. True prophets are always looking for the One they are called to point to and acknowledge, preparing His way and making it straight.

The Blood Must Be Applied

Moreover, they shall take some of the blood and put it on the two doorposts and on the lintel of the houses in which they eat it (Ex. 12:7).

The angel of death could not touch the houses that had the lamb's blood applied to them. Without the blood, they would have been doomed to the same judgement that came upon Egypt. It is by the application of the blood of Jesus to our lives that we are freed from God's judgement against the world and its sin, the wages of that sin being death. Nothing more, or less, will save us.

It would not have done Israel any good to know that there had to be the sacrifice of the Passover lamb or even to sacrifice it *unless they also applied it's blood to their houses.* Likewise, it will not benefit us to just know that there had to be a propitiation for our sins — it will not even do us any good to know that Jesus made that propitiation — *unless His blood is applied to our life.* To just know facts without applying them accomplishes nothing. Even demons know and believe the doctrine of salvation. It is not knowing in our minds, but believing in our hearts, which brings salvation (see Rom. 10:9-10).

The Lord explained through Moses that *"the life is in the blood"* (Lev. 17:11). It is only by the application of the Life of Jesus to our lives that we are saved: *"We were reconciled to God through the death of His Son, much more, having been reconciled, WE SHALL BE SAVED BY HIS LIFE"* (Rom. 5:10). The simple recognition of historic facts or understanding spiritual principles does not accomplish this; His life must be applied to our lives.

Because knowledge has so often been substituted for life, many have been made to feel comfortable in a spiritual condition in which they remain lost. Just having knowledge does not mean that it has been applied. Thomas a'Kempis wrote, "I would rather feel contrition than know the definition thereof . . . For what good does it do a man to be able to discourse profoundly concerning the Trinity, but lack humility and thereby be displeasing to the Trinity?"

There has been a great increase of knowledge during these last days, including spiritual knowledge. It has come because we are going to need every bit of it to accomplish the mandate the Lord has given us for this day. But the substituting of knowledge *for* life has led to much of the shallowness and lack of power in the church today. Knowledge only puffs up unless it leads to transformation and life. The Way is not a formula, but a Person. Truth is not just the assimilation and comprehension of spiritual facts but a Person. Unless we have come to know Jesus as our Life, we do not really know the Way or the Truth either.

The miracles performed by the Lord were not done just to impress us with His power; they were also meant to convey a message. His first miracle is the first one we need to understand. By it He was showing His newly gathered disciples the initial work to be done in them. At the wedding at Cana, the Lord ordered the vessels set aside. These vessels were typical of the disciples. He then had them filled with water, which is typical of the Word of God. Then He turned that water into wine, testifying of the fact that the Word would be changed into Spirit and Life. Once we have tasted this wine we will never again be satisfied with mere water. He has some who have allowed Him to fill them to the brim, and even then they have not gone out to serve it; they have waited patiently until the Lord has turned that water into the finest wine. This is what Paul meant when he said that *"when it pleased the Father to reveal His Son in me (not just to him) then I preached"* (Gal. 1:16).

Paul explained how the blood was applied to his life when he declared: *"I have been crucified with Christ; and it is no longer I who live, but Christ who lives in me"* (Gal. 2:20). Salvation is more than just forgiveness for sinful actions; it is deliverance from the indwelling evil that causes those actions! The crucifixion of Jesus accomplished an exchange for us — our body of death for His resurrection life. It is true we must die to our lives, interests and will to partake of Him; but no creature in all of creation will ever make a more profitable transaction.

We Must Eat the Flesh

And they shall eat the flesh the same night, roasted with fire, and they shall eat it with unleavened bread and bitter herbs (Ex. 12:8).

Jesus therefore said to them, "Truly, truly, I say to you, unless you eat of the flesh of the Son of Man and drink His blood, you have no life in yourselves. He who eats My flesh and drinks My blood has eternal life; and I will raise him up on the last day. For My flesh is true food, and My blood is true drink. He who eats My flesh and drinks My blood abides in Me, I in him. As the living Father sent Me, and I live because of the Father, so he who eats Me, he also shall live because of Me" (John 6:53-57).

"We are what we eat" is a common axiom. If we are partaking of the Lord Jesus, the Tree of Life, we will become that Life. Jesus did not say "he who has eaten My flesh" but "he who *eats*". This speaks of our need to continually partake of Him to abide in Him. He is the true Manna from Heaven (John 6:58). Just as Israel had to gather fresh manna each day because it would spoil if stored, so we too must seek Him afresh each day. We cannot be sustained on day old revelation. We cannot set aside one day to be spiritual and expect to abide in Him the rest of the week. He must be new to us every morning.

When the Lord referred to the eating of His flesh and drinking of His blood, of course He was not talking of His physical flesh and blood, but of what they symbolically represented — His life and His body, the church (we are bone of His bone and flesh of His flesh). Perplexed by what He said, most of those who heard this departed from Him (John 6:66). Confused leaders of the Church later reduced this truth to the destructive ritual of the Eucharist. What Jesus refers to is a *reality*, not just a ritual. To partake of the ritual is not equivalent to partaking of Him. The ritual of the Lord's supper was given as a reminder, not a substitute. When this ritual usurped the reality, the very life of the Lord was removed from the church, and she then plunged into the Dark Ages — an appropriate title for the spiritual depravity of those times.

The apostle Paul explained the meaning of this ritual to the Corinthians: *"The cup of blessing which we bless, is it not the communion of the blood of Christ? The bread which we break, is it not the communion of the body of Christ?"* (I Cor. 10:16 KJV). Communion was originally two words which were merged to form one — *COMMON* and *UNION*. This translates from the Greek *KOINONIA*, which is defined as: "The using of a thing in common". It is not the bread and wine that brings us together, but what they symbolically represent the blood and body of Jesus. The ritual we call communion is not an *actual* communion; it is a symbolic testimony that those partaking of it have a *common - union* in Christ. Jesus is our communion. He binds us together. The ritual simply designates the Purveyor of the bond. As Paul warned the Corinthians:

For I received from the Lord that which I also delivered to you, that the Lord Jesus in the night in which He was betrayed took bread;

*and when He had given thanks, He broke it and said, "This is My body, which is for you; do this in **REMEMBRANCE** of Me".*

*In this same way He took the cup also, after supper, saying, "This cup is the new covenant in My blood; do this, as often as you drink it, in **REMEMBRANCE** of Me".*

For as often as you eat this bread and drink the cup, you **proclaim** *the Lord's death until He comes.*

Therefore, whoever eats the bread or drinks the cup of the Lord in an unworthy manner, shall be guilty of the body and blood of the Lord.

But let a man examine himself and so let him eat of the bread and drink of the cup.

For he who eats and drinks, eats and drinks judgement to himself if he does not judge the body rightly.

For this reason many among you are weak and sick, and a number sleep (1 Cor. 11:23-30).

If we do not discern the body of Christ rightly we are pronouncing judgement upon ourselves when we partake of the bread and wine. That is, if we participate in the ritual assuming it fulfills our obligation to commune with Christ, we have deceived ourselves; we remain deprived of true Life. The substitution of rituals for realities has pervasively deprived men of redemption and salvation. *"For this reason many are weak, and sick, and a number sleep."* If a member of our physical body was cut off from the rest of the body, it would become weak, sick and die very fast. The same happens when we cut ourselves off from our spiritual body, the church. As the apostle John declared: *"If we walk in the light as He Himself is in the light, we have fellowship* (Greek "Koinonia": communion) *with one another, and the blood of His Son cleanses us from all sin"*. The Lord said "the life is in the blood". If we have "commune" with Him, we are joined in one Body under the Head, and His life's blood can flow through us.

Being properly joined to the body of Christ is not an option if true life is going to flow through us. But let us not substitute being joined to the body with being joined to the Head. By many, modern, popular definitions of what it means to be joined to the body, it has become possible, and even common, to be joined to the body without even having a relationship to the Head. Much of the church's emphasis over the last half of the twentieth century has been on being joined to the body, with very little emphasis on our being joined to the Head. If one is properly joined to the Head he will be properly joined to the body also, but the reverse is not necessarily true. We must not continue to get the cart in front of the horse in this issue.

Of course there have been many to use the excuse that they were seeking the Lord to avoid having a relationship to the church. As Peter related that "the unstable and untaught" distort teaching as well as the scriptures, there will be many who distort even the most sound doctrine. This is not an "either/or" issue. We must esteem our personal relationship to the Lord first, and also be properly related to His body if we are to have life. He said that we must "eat His flesh" *and* "drink His blood".

We Must Eat the Whole Thing

> *Do not eat any of it raw or boiled at all with water, but rather roasted with fire, both its head and entrails. And you shall not leave any of it over until morning* (Ex. 12:9-10).

Some have become very particular about the gospel, as if it were up to them to choose the aspects of redemption they need. If we are to partake of the Lord's Passover, we must accept every part of Him. He did not give us the option to take what we want. As He stated in the parable, when we find the pearl of great price, we must buy the whole field in which it was found.

When the Lord commissioned His followers to go and make disciples of all nations, He specifically included *"teaching them to observe ALL that I commanded you"* (Matt. 28:20). When we come with preconditions of what we will accept, we void the very power of the gospel. Often it is that which represents the greatest threat to us that we need the most.

The specific matter that intimidates us is not the important issue; to pick and choose what *we* want is an abdication of His Lordship. He cannot be received as Savior unless He also comes as Lord. It is the abdication to His Lordship that delivers us from the self-centeredness that kills us. Those who claim to have received Him as Savior but continue to live according to their own will are deceived. True salvation is the deliverance from self-will and our self-life in exchange for His life. If He is not the Lord *of* all, He is not the Lord *at* all.

When we compromise the gospel to make it acceptable or for any other reason, we strip it of the power to save. Deliverance from the power of evil is not accomplished by making a few changes. It is accomplished by deliverance from the "I WILL" that is rooted in our fallen nature, and the continual attempts we make to build our own towers to heaven.

Satan's original and most successful temptation has been that we could be "like God" (Gen. 3:5). Man's most destructive error is his determination to be his own lord! The whole world esteems and emulates "self-made" men. If one is self-made, he has thwarted his purpose for existence, to *be made* in the image of his Creator. Self-made men are supreme failures. "What will it profit a man to gain the whole world and lose his soul?" The Passover sacrifice of Jesus did not just "paint over" us with His blood; it cleansed us to destroy the angel of death, the body of sin and our self-will. Any gospel that preaches salvation without complete surrender is without salvation as well and is an enemy of the true gospel. A compromised gospel only immunizes us to the truth so that we cannot receive it when it comes to us.

> *"For whoever wishes to save his life shall lose it; but whoever loses his life for My sake shall find it"* (Matt. 16:25).

If we want His life, we must be willing to share His death. When the Lord called a man, he had to leave everything: *"So therefore, no one of you can be My disciple who does not give up all of his own possessions"* (Luke 14:33). Whether He requires this of us literally or just in our heart, it must be real and total. We must all experience the lessons of Job who had to lose everything but the Lord before he knew that the Lord was all he needed. A man who stands in need of nothing but Jesus will not be bound by anything or anyone but Him.

The Church today is fragmented. We have assumed the freedom to choose for ourselves which parts of the body of Christ we will accept. We naturally gravitate toward that which is most comfortable. The result has been a debilitating imbalance in most congregations. Those with an evangelistic burden are found in one group; those with a pastoral burden in another; the prophets in still another; one congregation is all "feet", another "hands" and another "eyes". These bodies are grotesque substitutes for the perfect body Christ is determined to have. Each member must be properly joined to the others if the Body is to function rightly. Even if one is a perfect heart, what good would that heart be if it did not have the lungs, kidneys, liver, etc. Presently we have all hearts in one place claiming to be the body, all livers in another, and so forth. There must be interchange, interrelationship, and the proper joining of the different parts of the body before there can be an effective functioning of the same.

Pastors have a God-given cautious nature that is protective of the flock of God. Prophets are visionary by nature. Without the balance and influence of the prophetic ministry, pastors will tend to stagnate and become set in their ways. Without the influence of pastors, prophets will drift into extremes, having visions which no one knows how to practically fulfill. Teachers will be pragmatic in nature, which is essential for clear impartation of the word, but without prodding from the other ministries they tend to reduce the life in Christ to principles and formulas that are learned by rote. Evangelists are given to focus on the needs of the lost, often forgetting to raise and mature them, but without evangelists the Church will quickly forget the unsaved. Because apostles are called to be evangelists, prophets, pastors and teachers, they usually have a more balanced nature, and are given for the purpose of keeping the Church on the right path. The unity of the Spirit is not a unity by conformity: it is a unity of diversity. For this reason the Lord gave apostles, prophets, evangelists, pastors and teachers to equip the saints (Eph. 4:11-12). We must receive *all* the ministries. To partake of the Lord's body, we must "eat the whole thing".

We are exhorted to *"grow up in all aspects unto Him, Who is the Head"* (Eph. 4:15). The apostles were directed to *"speak to the people in the temple the whole message of this Life"* (Acts 5:20). The psalmist discerned that *"the SUM of Thy word is truth"* (Ps. 119:160). We can be distracted from the Truth by individual truths. We can be distracted from the River of Life by the individual tributaries which feed it. Almost every denomination is built around a single emphasis. They may teach other aspects, but emphasize one small portion of the whole revelation of God. Any time we focus our attention on one part of the whole, our scope will be limited. Only when we focus on the Truth (Jesus) do all truths take their proper perspective. Jesus is the sum of God's word.

Until we see Jesus as the summation of all spiritual truth, we are like the proverbial blind men trying to comprehend the elephant: one thought it was a tree because he had found its leg; another thought it was a fan because he had found an ear; another thought it was a whip because he had found the tail, and so it goes. When we see the whole animal, we understand that they were all correct but in fact would be deceived about the true nature of the elephant until they perceived the whole thing. Individual aspects of God's word may be interpreted falsely apart from the whole Word. The Lord emphasized the fact that the scriptures have eternal life in them only if they testify of Him (John 5:39-40). Overbalance in one area is indicative of partial, incomplete comprehension of the whole. As Paul explained to the Hebrews: *"God, after He spoke long ago to the fathers in the prophets in many portions and many ways, in these last days has spoken to us in His Son"* (Heb. 1:1-2). The Father is no longer giving us fragments. He has given us the whole Loaf.

We may have such a vision of the united and perfected Body of Christ that we are sure this Church will draw all men to itself. But the church is not to draw men, but to minister to them and equip them once they have been drawn. It is only when Jesus is lifted up that men will be drawn together, and they will be drawn to HIM! King David perceived this and wrote the "Psalm of Unity" (Psalm 133): *"Behold how good and pleasant it is for brothers to dwell together in unity! It is like precious oil UPON THE HEAD (Jesus), coming down upon the beard . . . coming down upon the edge of his robes"*. If we anoint the Head with our worship and devotion, the oil will run down and cover the whole body (of Christ). There will one day be a Church that is perfected in unity, but it is likely that she will not even be aware of it. Her attention will be on Jesus, not herself.

We Must Eat in Haste

Now you shall eat it in this manner: with your loins girded, your

*sandals on your feet, and your staff in your hand; and you shall
eat it in HASTE* (Ex. 12:11).

Included in the Passover was The Feast of Unleavened Bread
(Ex. 12:14-20). For seven days (beginning with the first day of the
Passover), Israel could not eat any leavened bread. This was meant
to remind the Israelites of their flight from Egypt, when they left in
such haste that their bread did not have time to become leavened:

*And they baked the dough which they had brought out of Egypt
into cakes of unleavened bread. For it had not become leavened, since they were driven out of Egypt and could not delay*
(Ex. 12:39).

Because of its permeating characteristics, leaven (yeast) is
symbolic of sin in scripture:

*Do you not know that a little leaven leavens the whole lump of
dough?*

*Clean out the old leaven, that you may be a new lump, just as
in fact you are unleavened. For Christ our Passover also has
been sacrificed.*

*Let us therefore celebrate the feast, not with old leaven, nor
with the leaven of malice and wickedness, but with the unleavened bread of sincerity and truth* (1 Cor. 5:6-8).

Leaven is also symbolic of doctrine that is legalistic in nature.
The Lord warned His disciples to *"Beware of the leaven of the
Pharisees and Sadducees"* (Matt. 16:6). Not long after the gospel
began to spread, converts from the Pharisees tried to bring the
young Church under the yoke of the Law. Satan was trying to
seduce the young bride of Christ with the same deception used to
seduce the bride of the first Adam: eat of the Tree of The Knowledge of Good and Evil. After great controversy, the apostles and
elders sent word to all of the churches in what was a most important and historical communique.

*For it seemed good to the Holy Spirit and to us to lay upon you
no greater burden than these essentials:*

*that you abstain from things strangled and from fornication; if
you keep yourselves free from such things, you will do well*
(Acts 15:28-29).

Webster's New World Dictionary defines leaven as "a substance
such as yeast used to produce fermentation, especially in dough".
The same dictionary defines fermentation as "a state of excitement;
agitation; commotion; unrest". The apostles and elders in Jerusalem
noted that the Pharisee converts produced the same characteristics
in the Church: *"Since we have heard that some of our number to
whom we gave no instruction, have **disturbed** you with their words,
unsettling your souls"* (Acts 15:24). Such are the characteristics of
spiritual leaven.

Doctrines that disturb and unsettle the body of Christ are often
rooted in legalism. There is a continual pressure upon the Church
to walk in principles and/or formulas to gain maturity. These
doctrines usually seem "good for food, a delight to the eyes, and
desirable to make one wise" (Gen. 3:6). Satan could not tempt us
if the fruit were not appealing. Laws, principles and formulas are
appealing because they offer the security of a known commodity.
Walking by law or principles gives us the control that our insecurity
demands. But this is a false security. It is security in oneself rather
than the One in Whom alone there is true security.

*"For all who are being led by the Spirit of God, these are the sons
of God"* (Rom. 8:14). As discussed earlier, walking by the Spirit
does not mean that we do not keep the Law. If we walk by the
Spirit we do more than keep the Law; we fulfill it! For example, the
law says we are not to covet our neighbor's wife or property. The
Spirit calls us to an even higher way, to love our neighbor. If we
love our neighbor, of course we will not covet what is his, nor in
any way do him harm. The Spirit does not just command: He
imparts the ability to love . . . He imparts His love. Jesus did not
come to destroy the Law but to fulfill it — He came to lift us **above**
the Law; He came to give us the power to exceed its requirements.

Walking in the Spirit is life, peace and fulfillment, but it is
difficult. It is difficult because the flesh wars against the Spirit. The

"I WILL" nature of Cain within us will not easily submit to the Spirit. There is a determination in the flesh to "be as God" and to rule its own destiny. This determination to control desperately resists relinquishing control. But if we are to live by the Spirit, Jesus alone must be our Master.

It is easier to make rules than to be sensitive to the Spirit. Regulations can bring order and relieve many pressures, but they cannot change the inner man. A time is coming when the regulations will not be able to cope with the chaos. We must have a more solid foundation. If we are seeking order and security in our religion, we will lose both.

The fear of deception will not keep one from deception: it will lead to it. We must not walk by fear but by faith. The scripture testifies that the only thing that will keep us from deception is to have a *love for the Truth,* Himself. When we open our shades at night, darkness does not come in, light shines out into the darkness. Light overcomes darkness because it is more powerful. If we seek to do our Father's will and serve Him, we will find an order and security that no degree of chaos can overcome. We must be able to hear and distinguish His voice from all the other voices in the world. When the shaking comes, and it will (Heb. 12:25-29), knowing His voice and following Him will be the only true security we have, and it is the greatest security we can have.

Does this mean that we should do away with all laws, rules, and regulations in society? Certainly not! As the apostle explained: *"But we know that the law is good if one uses it lawfully, realizing the fact that the law was not made for the righteous man* (those in Christ), *but for those who are lawless and rebellious, for the ungodly and sinners, for the unholy and profane"* (1 Tim. 1:8-9). In the world, laws and regulations are necessary to maintain a semblance of order until the kingdom comes, but they must not be imposed for spiritual discipline; only the Spirit can beget that which is spirit.

The Bible is God's instruction book for the human being. It contains the greatest wisdom ever written in the human language. It gives important instructions about how the human really works, concerning both our potential and what causes our problems. It would be impossible to put a value on this most marvelous gift the Lord has given to us, but the Bible was given to lead us *to* Jesus, *not* to take His place.

The Lord says amazingly less than one would think concerning order in the Church (for a good reason). It is essential for His sheep to know His voice. The Church must be ruled and guided by the Head rather than by formulas. He is purposely vague concerning even important issues so that we have to seek Him. The New Testament is full of the best counsel the world has ever heard, but the Lord and His apostles were careful not to lay down many general rules and regulations for the churches. They knew that every rule could prevent that church from seeking the Lord for themselves.

Developing the relationship with Him is the important work that the Spirit is doing in us. He was sent to lead us to Jesus. Used as a rulebook, the Bible becomes the letter that kills, the Tree of Knowledge, and can even become an idol. Used properly, it turns us to Him and helps us to walk with Him, abide in Him, and know Him, not just about Him.

The Pharisees confronted every problem with a new rule. The Lord referred to their doctrines as leaven because they caused agitation and commotion among the people. When we try to confront problems in the Church with new regulations, we are sowing leaven. Like the doctrines of the Pharisees, these only clean up the outside; they are not able to deal with the true problem. They may bring a degree of control and order, but the greatest order one can find among people is in the cemetery! When order takes the place of having a relationship with the Lord that is usually what we end up with — a spiritual cemetery. The dead don't cause any problems. The spiritually dead will have an orderly church. But the Lord came to give *abundant* life. Abundance does not dictate that it be all good; it just means there is a lot of it! It includes the good and the bad.

Living by regulations will give outward order but it will breed agitation and unrest in spirit. There is no true rest in the law until there is death, making men machines or zombies instead of humans who are able to have a relationship with their Creator. Jesus is "the Lord of the Sabbath", or the Lord of rest. Abiding in Him we have Life and peace. He says to us: *"Cease striving and know that I AM God"* (Ps. 46:10). The Law makes us look at ourselves where we will only see death and corruption. The Spirit shows us Jesus and Life which creates a love and yearning that keeps us always in pursuit of Him.

"The unfolding of Thy word gives light" says the Psalmist (Ps. 119:130). There is unfathomable depth of revelation we have not yet realized in God's Word, even concerning the most basic doctrines. It is a terrible mistake to become satisfied with our present knowledge and understanding. We all are seeing through a glass darkly. We cannot know anything fully until we know Him fully. *"The path of the righteous is like the light of dawn, that shines brighter and brighter until the full day"* (Prov. 4:18). When the truth stops expanding for us, we begin to live in darkness.

Water is often used symbolically as the Word of God in scripture (see Eph. 5:26). When the Lord uses a natural type to symbolize a spiritual reality, it is because its characteristics reflect the nature of the spiritual. One important characteristic of water is that it must keep flowing in order to stay pure. Once it settles into one place it becomes stagnant very fast, and so does the Word of God. Every revelation of truth in our life should be continually expanding and deepening for us. That's why the river of life is just that — a river! It is not a pond or a lake; it is flowing, moving, going somewhere. As an old sage once remarked, "You can never step into the same river twice."

Having truth that expands is threatening to those who are of the spirit of the Pharisees, who have a zeal for the Lord and desire for purity of truth but whose real security is in fact in human traditions with which they insolate the truth. With those who are of this spirit, there will be a defacto elevating of orthodoxy to the same level as biblical revelation, even though they would vehemently deny that this is so. When we understand that there is much more to be understood and we are seeking deeper understanding concerning a doctrine, there *is* the potential for erroneous revelation. If we do not seek deeper revelation, we already have error that is debilitating and poisonous. **Having truth will not keep one from deception, but having *a love for the truth* will.**

Israel's bread did not have time to become leavened because they left Egypt in such haste. If we too will keep moving on with the Spirit, our bread will not have time to become leavened with sin, wickedness, or legalism. It's when we stop moving and growing that our "bread" becomes infected.

In the section "**Taking The Lamb Into The House**", we discussed how the Passover lamb was taken into the houses of Israel to be thoroughly examined for five days before the sacrifice, and how this may reflect the need for one to thoroughly examine Christ before making a commitment. But we see here that once the commitment is made, we must then move in haste to flee the land of Egypt.

It is interesting to note that *immediately* after one believed in the early church he was baptized. This speaks of the need not to force or rush a decision out of a person, but once a true commitment is made, it needs to be sealed at once with the biblical ordinance given for the public demonstration of faith — water baptism. Nowhere in scripture do we find such things as an altar call, the raising of hands, or the myriad of other customs we have substituted for the biblical rite of immediate baptism. These human devices, which have been instituted mostly for the sake of convenience, have proven counter-productive in sealing the commitment of the new believer. How much more impact would the "decision" have on new converts if we faithfully complied with the biblical mandate for immediate baptism. How much more would their commitment stand as a powerful road mark in their lives if they could see a biblical testimony of their action, in place of the vague wonder if anything really happened after a walk down an isle or the brief raising of their hands?

No Strangers May Eat Of It

This is the ordinance of the Passover: no STRANGER may eat of it (Ex. 12:43).

As the Church grows in the grace and knowledge of our Lord, we will become more tolerant, but this does not mean we will be all-inclusive. History testifies that each restoration of truth to the church is vulnerable to getting diluted or stamped out by the multitude. Our tendency to seek security through the approval of numbers has cost the church immeasurably by watering down the power of the pure and uncompromised truth. We are warned to beware when all men think well of us. Did people not heartily hail the false prophets? (Luke 6:26) We must be secure only in the justification and approval of God. *"The fear of man is a snare"* (Prov. 29:25).

A door has two functions: to let people in and to keep them out. Jesus is the Door. When we allow those to join the church who have not come through the Door, we place both the congregation and the unconverted in jeopardy. This is not to say these should not be allowed to attend services or meetings, but that they should not be included as a member of the Body of Christ until they have been joined to the Head.

New buildings, family life centers, projects and programs have drawn many into the churches. They may have also helped to keep some in churches, but they have never drawn a man to Christ. We may even think that the dynamic spirituality of our fellowship will bring men to Him, but it never will. The church can actually be a distraction and hindrance to true conversion if it allows membership in the church without rebirth in Jesus. Mere church attendance and activism can work to appease the conviction the Holy Spirit is seeking to bring into one's life and may enable one to feel safe in a spiritual condition in which he remains lost.

The first thing which God said was *not good* was for man to be alone. He made us social creatures and therefore we all crave strong social ties. The true Church is the most dynamic social entity the world has ever known. We must be careful that people are not drawn to our assemblies instead of to the Lord. It is common for people to say the right things, change their outward behavior and even sincerely believe the doctrine of Christ in their minds but without knowing Jesus in their heart. It is possible to be quite "spiritual" and not know Him, as the Lord Himself testified.

> *Many will say to Me on that day, "Lord, Lord, did we not prophesy in Your name, and in your name cast out demons, and in Your name perform many miracles?" And I will say to them, "I never knew you; depart from Me you who practice lawlessness"* (Matt. 7:22-23).

"The branch cannot bear fruit of itself, unless it abides in the vine, so neither can you unless you abide in Me" (John 15:4). To be joined to the Church through Christ is life and power. Seeking union with Christ through the Church is vain. One cannot be joined to Christ

without being joined to His Body. We have often made it easy for one to be attached to the body without being joined to the Head. Paul scrupulously presented Christ crucified to the unsaved. He understood that if people were drawn by anything but Jesus the conversion could be false. Paul used no psychology or methodology. He used something much more powerful — THE GOSPEL.

There is great danger in "not discerning the body rightly" and allowing those to join with us who have not come through the Door. It is also dangerous to presume knowledge of another's spiritual condition or his standing before God when it is not *obvious.* There are certain basic truths we must agree on in order to walk together, essentially the atonement and Lordship of Jesus. When we become exclusive based on our doctrines which go beyond the revelation of Jesus as the Door, we are in danger of cutting ourselves off from the Body of Christ and becoming a sect or even a cult.

The Tabernacle of Moses was a type of both the Lord Jesus and the Church, as both were to be the habitation of God. In Moses' Tabernacle, the closer one came to the presence of the Lord, the more sanctified he was required to be. Our situation is similar. The apostle exhorts: *"Pursue peace with all men* (tolerance), *and the sanctification* (separation) *without which no one will see the Lord"* (Heb. 12:14).

When the Tabernacle of Moses was constructed and sanctified for use, an unsanctified man could not enter the Holy Place or even look upon the furniture inside. The penalty for this was death (Num. 4:20). This was to testify of the requirement of sanctification before we can see the most holy things. If one is living in darkness and is suddenly exposed to great light, he will not be enlightened; He will be blinded! Because of this we must be discerning when exposing unbelievers, or new believers, to the deeper truths of the Lord. Meat will not nourish babies; it will choke them.

Because acacia wood was twisted, knotty and hard to work with, it is often typical of fallen human nature in scripture. In the Outer Court of the Tabernacle of Moses, the furniture was made of natural, exposed, acacia wood and was illumined by the natural light of the sun. This testified of the fact that most who just enter the Outer Court usually have their sinful nature exposed and walk more by the "natural" light.

Entering the Tabernacle we come into the Holy Place. The furniture here is also made of acacia wood, but it is covered in pure gold. Gold, being incorruptible, is symbolic of the Divine nature. The only light in the Holy Place is provided by olive oil burned in a lampstand, the olive oil being typical of the anointing of the Holy Spirit. In the Holy Place there is no natural light, and we cannot function there with our natural minds but are dependent on the Holy Spirit. In the Holy of Holies, the innermost compartment where the Lord Himself dwells, the mercy seat is gold inside and out. The light provided in the Holy of Holies is the very Presence of the Lord. We see by this that the closer one gets to the glory of the Lord, the more gold there is, typifying the fact that we are changed into the Divine nature by the glory (see 2 Cor. 3:18). As we get closer to the glory, the light by which we walk changes from natural light to the anointing of the Holy Spirit to the very presence and glory of the Lord.

"Our God is a consuming fire" (Heb. 12:29). Had the acacia wood been exposed to the fire of God's glory without being covered by the gold, it would have been consumed. Sanctification is required to see the Lord and to draw close to Him for our sake, lest we be consumed (Heb. 12:14).

Unfortunately, many have a concept of the Father as being the God of the Old Testament who would destroy us if Jesus did not mediate and assuage His wrath. We must not forget that it was the Father who sent His Son because He "so loved the world". The Father Himself loves us, and desires fellowship with us so much that He submitted His own Son to torture and death so that we could draw near to Him. But God is holy, and His holiness is a consuming fire. That is why sanctification is required to see Him. If we are still wood, hay and stubble, we will be consumed by His presence. It is only as we have come to more fully abide in His Son, being covered by more and more of the gold of His divine nature, that we are able to draw closer and closer to the Father. It was the crucifixion of Jesus that rent the veil which separated us from the Father. It is as we are "crucified with Christ", when His cleansing blood has been applied to life, that the way is made for us to boldly enter into the Father's presence which is His heart's desire.

The ministry in the Outer Court is to the people. The ministry in the Holy Place and Holy of Holies is to the Lord. This is what transforms us. Without this ministry to the Lord, we will not be as effective in our Outer Court ministry. We must carry light from the Lord, but we cannot take the people into that light until they have been sanctified. No strangers may partake of the Passover of the Lord, and one who has not discerned the Body rightly should not partake of the bread and wine.

Just as there were three dimensions to the tabernacle ministry, the Lord had three basic levels to His ministry: to the multitude, the twelve and then the three. He spoke to the multitudes in parables and basics (the Outer Court). To the twelve He revealed the mysteries, and they experienced the anointing (Holy Place). The three were privileged to see His glory on the Mount of Transfiguration (Holy Of Holies). Pastors who are evangelical in orientation will have congregations which focus mostly on the Outer Court aspect of the ministry. Pastors who are teacher oriented will tend to have congregations which emphasize the ministry typified by the Holy Place. Those led by prophets will seek to abide in the Holy of Holies. The properly balanced congregations will have a ministry on all three levels as the Lord and the tabernacle exemplify.

Every congregation and minister needs to have an outreach to the lost and ministry to those at every level of maturity. Failure to do so usually leads to imbalance and often error. If we do not have new converts, there will be stagnation. If we do not have meetings that are devoted entirely to worshipping the Lord without the distraction of human pressure, demands, and even needs, there will be shallowness and a lack of anointing and power for the ministry to the people.

Recognizing the importance of providing ministry for all levels of maturity is essential, but we must understand that it is wrong to distinguish and value people by their level of maturity. The purpose for each level of ministry was to prepare those in that place for the next higher level. If the ministry is functioning properly, everyone will be maturing and entering higher levels of experience, effectiveness and intimacy with the Lord Himself. Those in ministry need to discern where a person is in order to serve him effectively, not to label him as a certain class of Christian.

Some have taken this understanding of the levels of maturity to classify and distinguish themselves as superior or others as inferior. This cannot be helped. As Peter remarked concerning Paul's teachings, there were some things in them which were hard to understand, which the unstable and untaught distorted, just as they did the rest of the scriptures (see 2 Pet. 3:15-16). Pride in a man's heart will cause him to use even the scriptures to feed his ego. If true humility is in one's character, even the greatest accolades of God and man will but further humble him.

True humility is not an inferiority complex. True humility comes from seeing the majesty of the Lord. As the apostle explained, those who measure themselves by themselves (or with each other) were without understanding (2 Cor. 10:12). In His kingdom, the purpose of authority and position is for serving. The faithful and obedient ministry of helps is more esteemed with God than the most noteworthy apostle who considers himself higher than others.

There will be tares growing among the wheat in the church. Even the apostle Paul ordained elders who would prove to be wolves (see Acts 20:29-30). Jesus chose Judas and included him in the inner circle. Though these may cause great damage and confusion, they are actually working out the purposes of God. All things work for the good of those who love God. Such disruptions almost always result in our becoming more dependent on the Lord, and less dependent on those who are but flesh and blood. This is not to say we should purposely ordain traitors and include false brethren in our assemblies, but that it will happen and it will work out for our good.

During the 1960's and 70's, there was a major emphasis upon "submission" in the Body of Christ. This was a word from God and only He knows how badly we needed it because of the rebellion then surfacing in the world. But we quickly formed our doctrines on submission and started judging men by how well they conformed to the doctrine instead of looking for the fruit of submission in their lives. As a result of this, some of the most unbroken and rebellious ministries were released upon the church because they conformed to the doctrine of submission. Likewise, some of the most truly broken and submissive men and women of God were almost blackballed from ministry because they did not conform to the doctrine. The devastation caused by this shallowness is now history.

In the coming years, "humility" will become an emphasis. This is a timely and important word, but let us not make the same mistake with it that we did with submission. The Lord does resist the proud and gives grace to the humble, but it is so much better when we let Him do it. We must start to know one another after the Spirit and not after the flesh. Only the Spirit can judge accurately. Appearances are almost always deceiving. King Saul appeared humble; it was said that he was "small in his own eyes". David appeared arrogant and insolent, rebuking the armies of Israel for their timidity and saying that the King's own armor was not good enough for him. We must rise above the tendency to follow the first one who appears to be head and shoulders above the rest.

Those whom we judge as tares by our own understanding may well be wheat and vice versa. That is why the Lord instructed us to let the wheat and tares grow together until the harvest. Until there is maturity, the wheat and tares may look so much alike that it will be almost impossible to tell them apart. Both may be arrogant; they may both even have false concepts or teaching or fall into sin occasionally. The difference will only be obvious when they both mature. During the harvest, wheat will bow over, while the tares remain standing upright. When wheat matures, it becomes humble, but those who are in fact tares will continue in their pride.

Let us also not forget God's grace or judgement. Some who are tares may repent and become wheat. Likewise, some who are wheat will fall and become stumbling blocks in our midst. That "no strangers are to partake of the Passover" is a truth, but let us be careful how we apply it. Those who have not entered through the Door are obvious. Judging beyond that is difficult and dangerous and can lead to grievous errors.

If we are walking in the Light, we will allow truth to remain at the point of Divine tension between the extremes and will refrain from making a formula, principle, or inflexible doctrine out of it. It is the fruit of the Tree of Knowledge which demands our carrying the paradoxes in scripture to their logical conclusions. The paradoxes are there to force us to seek the Lord for His mind and wisdom. This leads to our walking by the Spirit instead of principles or laws. By resisting the compulsion to make formulas and allowing truth to rest at the point of tension between the extremes, we begin to partake of the Tree of Life. Christianity is not just following a set of rules; it is walking with God.

Spoiling Egypt

Now the sons of Israel had done according to the word of Moses, for they had requested from the Egyptians articles of silver and articles of gold, and clothing;

and the Lord had given the people favor in the sight of the Egyptians, so that they let them have their request. Thus they plundered the Egyptians (Ex. 12:35-36).

After being slaves for four hundred years, Israel partook of the Passover and became more wealthy than their wildest imagination. When we partake of the true Passover which is Christ, in Him we are given the right to become the sons of God to Whom belongs the world and all it contains. Even so, all of the world's riches are as nothing compared to the spiritual riches that are in Christ. But just as it is written, *"Things which eye has not seen and ear has not heard, and which have not entered into the heart of man, all that God has prepared for those who love Him"* (1 Cor. 2:9). Truly, in Christ we have inherited more riches than we are capable of imagining.

Israel left Egypt weighted down with wealth, but they were not taken to the closest bazaar so they could spend it. He took them into the wilderness where they could not spend even a single shekel! There they were able to invest their riches for something more valuable than anything the world could sell them — the tabernacle, a habitation for God that He might dwell among them.

Today the Body of Christ receives a great deal of teaching about the riches we have in Christ. This teaching is timely. For centuries the Church has been deprived of the inheritance she has in Christ. Unfortunately this emphasis has often been devoted more to the material than the eternal. This is the delusion of slaves who one day dramatically find themselves kings. We have been removed from Egypt but Egypt has not yet been removed from us in many ways. However, it is encouraging that many are beginning to reject this mentality and envision the incomparable riches of Christ.

Blessed be the God and Father of our Lord Jesus Christ, who has blessed us with every spiritual blessing in the heavenly places in Christ (Eph. 1:3).

When we perceive our *spiritual* blessings in Christ, *material* blessings lose their appeal. If one were to discover a vein of gold that could provide all the world's needs forever, would he continue panning for mere nuggets? We have that vein in the Person of our Lord Jesus. Why do we give so much attention to the things which pass away? It is because we have not truly seen Him as He is; we have merely discovered a few things about Him.

In Hebrews 11 (popularly referred to as "the faith chapter"), there is a long list of the great triumphs of faith. These are wonderful testimonies of God's faithfulness to those who call upon Him in faith. Many deliverances are taking place today that are just as wonderful. But seldom is the last part of that chapter noted:

> *And others were tortured, **not accepting their release, in order that they might obtain a better resurrection;***
>
> *and others experienced mockings and scourgings, yes also chains and imprisonment.*
>
> *They were stoned, they were sawn in two, they were tempted, they were put to death with the sword; they went about in sheepskins, **being destitute**, afflicted, ill treated,*
>
> *men of whom the world was not worthy, wandering in deserts and mountains and caves and holes in the ground.*
>
> *And all these, having gained approval through their faith, did not receive what was promised,*
>
> *because God had provided something better for us, so that apart from us they should not be made perfect* (Heb. 11:35-40).

These who were seeking a "better resurrection" did not quench the power of fire or close the mouths of lions — they would not even accept their release! They did not live in palaces; they lived in holes in the ground and in caves. The Lord Jesus Himself did not even have a place to lay His head (Matt. 8:20). When we begin to see the spiritual riches in Christ, it will not matter to us where we live. If Jesus is in it, a cave will have more glory than the greatest human structure. To live in a cave or palace will make little difference if we abide in Him. Some think it is more spiritual to be abased and others that it is more spiritual to abound, but neither is true. We may be in error if we are trying to live an abased life that God has not called us to or vice versa. The issue is to be in the will of the Lord and to keep a steadfast devotion to Him whether we are abounding or being abased.

Cain was the father of those who are earthly minded; he was a "tiller of the ground". Those who are still carnal will always be seekers of earthly gain, regardless of the spiritual guise. The Kingdom of our Lord and His chosen is not of this world. Those who seek His kingdom are strangers and sojourners; here they have no lasting city and they are not trying to build one; they are seeking the city whose architect and builder is God.

This heart of the spiritual sojourner cannot be attained by seeking it. Those who seek to be unearthly for its own sake, believing it to spiritual, usually become sad examples of spiritual barrenness. *"The promises of God are, in Him, yea, and amen"* (2 Cor. 1:20). The promises of God are positives, not negatives. A failure to understand this is why some of the most worldly and unspiritual men are found in monasteries and secluded spiritual communities. (This is not to imply that all who are found in these are so.) The truly spiritual man is one because his heart is so captured by the things of the spirit that he simply has no time or interest for the things of the world. Once we have beheld the spiritual riches that are found in Christ, going back to worldly interests could be compared to a billionaire sweeping streets for minimum wages. Those who still have a love for worldly pleasures simply have not received the love of the Father (see 1 John 2:15). As Paul explained to the Colossians:

If you have died with Christ to the elementary principles of the world, why, as if you were living in the world, do you submit yourself to decrees, such as, "Do not handle, do not taste, do not touch!"

which all refer to things destined to perish with the using, in accordance with the commandments and teachings of men?

These are matters which have, to be sure, the appearance of wisdom in self-made religion and self-abasement and severe treatment of the body, but are of no value against fleshly indulgence. (Col. 2:20-23)

True spirituality is not just a distaste for the world and its interests; true spirituality is a consuming love for the things of the Spirit and the interests of our God. This can only come when the eyes of our heart have been opened so that the things of the Spirit are more real to us than the things which are seen with the eyes of our minds.

The Waving of the Sheaf

As a fitting last touch to this remarkable Feast of the Passover, the Lord instituted what is called "The Waving of the Sheaf of the Firstfruits". (See Lev. 23:5-15.) This feast was celebrated in early spring as the first shoots of the coming harvest were just sprouting. On the morning after the Passover Sabbath, a sheaf of this first evidence of the coming harvest was brought to the priest and he waved them before the Lord. As this ritual was being performed after the Passover of our Lord's crucifixion, Jesus was bursting forth from His tomb! Jesus was the Sheaf of the firstfruits of the resurrection, who at that very time was being waved before the Lord as evidence of the coming great harvest, perfectly fulfilling the type.

It is an interesting fact that more scripture is devoted to Abraham choosing a burial place for his family than on such important subjects as being born again or church order. Isaac and Jacob insisted on being buried there, and Joseph made the sons of Israel swear to carry his bones up from Egypt to bury Him there. It is a great enigma as to why the patriarchs give so much importance to where they are to be buried until we read Matt. 27:50-53.

And Jesus cried out again with a loud voice, and yielded up His spirit.

And behold, the veil of the temple was torn in two from top to bottom, and the earth shook; and the rocks were split, and the tombs were opened; and many bodies of the saints who had fallen asleep were raised;

and coming out of the tombs after His resurrection they entered the holy city and appeared to many.

The burial ground which Abraham had chosen for his family was just outside of Jerusalem. Abraham was a prophet who had foreseen the resurrection of Jesus as the Lord Himself confirmed, *"Your father Abraham rejoiced to see my day; and he saw it and was glad"* (John 8:56). Abraham and those of his family who had vision had made a provision to be a part of the first resurrection.

The patriarchs were not just concerned about where they were buried but when they would be raised. Those who have vision are also making provision by how they are buried as to how they will be raised. If we have been buried with Christ, we shall also be raised with Him (Rom. 6:5). Every Christian is called to be a martyr — everyday! We make provision for our resurrection every day by laying down our lives and being buried with Him. In the light of this, one of the great men of vision of all time gave the church what may be his most important exhortation:

For we are the true circumcision, who worship in the Spirit of God and glory in Christ Jesus and put no confidence in the flesh.

More than that, I count all things to be loss in view of the surpassing value of knowing Christ Jesus my Lord, for whom I have suffered the loss of all things, and count them but rubbish in order that I may gain Christ,

and may be found in Him, not having a righteousness of my own derived from the Law, but that which is through faith in Christ, the righteousness which comes from God on the basis of faith,

that I may know Him, and the power of His resurrection and the fellowship of His sufferings, being conformed to His death; in order that I may attain to the resurrection from the dead.

Not that I have already obtained it, or have already become perfect, but I press on in order that I may lay hold of that for which also I was laid hold of by Christ Jesus.

Brethren, I do not regard myself as having laid hold of it yet; but one thing I do: forgetting what lies behind and reaching forward to what lies ahead,

I press on toward the goal for the prize of the upward call of God in Christ Jesus (Phil. 3:3, 8-14).

When Paul declared *"one thing I do"*, it reflected the singleness of his mind on this issue. When our eye, or vision, is likewise single, our whole body will be full of light. Only then will we know true resurrection life and power.

Other Books Available From
MorningStar Publications

THE HARVEST by Rick Joyner. A sweeping prophetic scenario of the last days. Since its publication, events predicted in this vision have quickly begun to unfold. This book has been called "essential reading for those who are committed to discerning the times."

REALITY by Aaron Katz. This is a penetrating prophetic call to live in the *reality* of the things which are eternal. This is possibly one of the most challenging books written since Bonhoeffer's <u>The Cost Of Discipleship.</u>

THE HARVEST TRILOGY by Rick Joyner and Robert Burnell. This book contains the popular summary of <u>The Harvest</u> titled, "A Vision Of The Harvest," "The Titanic And The Stock Market" by Rick Joyner, and the classic allegory "Escape From Christendom" by Robert Burnell, all in one attractive paperback.

THE MORNING STAR 1988 – 1989. This book contains all of the articles and prophetic words published in <u>The Morning Star Prophetic Newsletter</u> during this two year period.

These books are available in your local Christian bookstore or you may write to:

MorningStar
P.O. Box 369
Pineville, NC. 28134

The Morning Star Prophetic Magazine

Co-edited by Rick Joyner and Francis Frangipane, this publication is devoted to serving the body of Christ "meat in due season," what the Spirit is presently saying to the church. It includes:

1. Teaching. In-depth studies by Rick, Francis and some of the most anointed teachers now serving the body of Christ.

2. Prophecy. A whole section devoted to what the Spirit is presently saying to the church, written by proven, recognized prophetic ministries.

3. Chronicles. The Acts of the last day church which are now taking place.

4. Intercession. This section is devoted to helping mobilize the "heavy artillery" of the Lord's last day army: the intercessory prayer teams.

5. Newsletter. This is a special section offered to ministries we believe have an important voice in the unfolding move of God.

6. Events. This includes notices of upcoming conferences and special meetings or events.

TO SUBSCRIBE: Send **$10.00** (U.S. dollars) to:

The Morning Star Magazine
P.O. Box 369
Pineville, NC. 28134

*Subscribers receive a **10% discount** on all books, tapes or other products distributed by MorningStar Publications for as long as their subscription is current.*